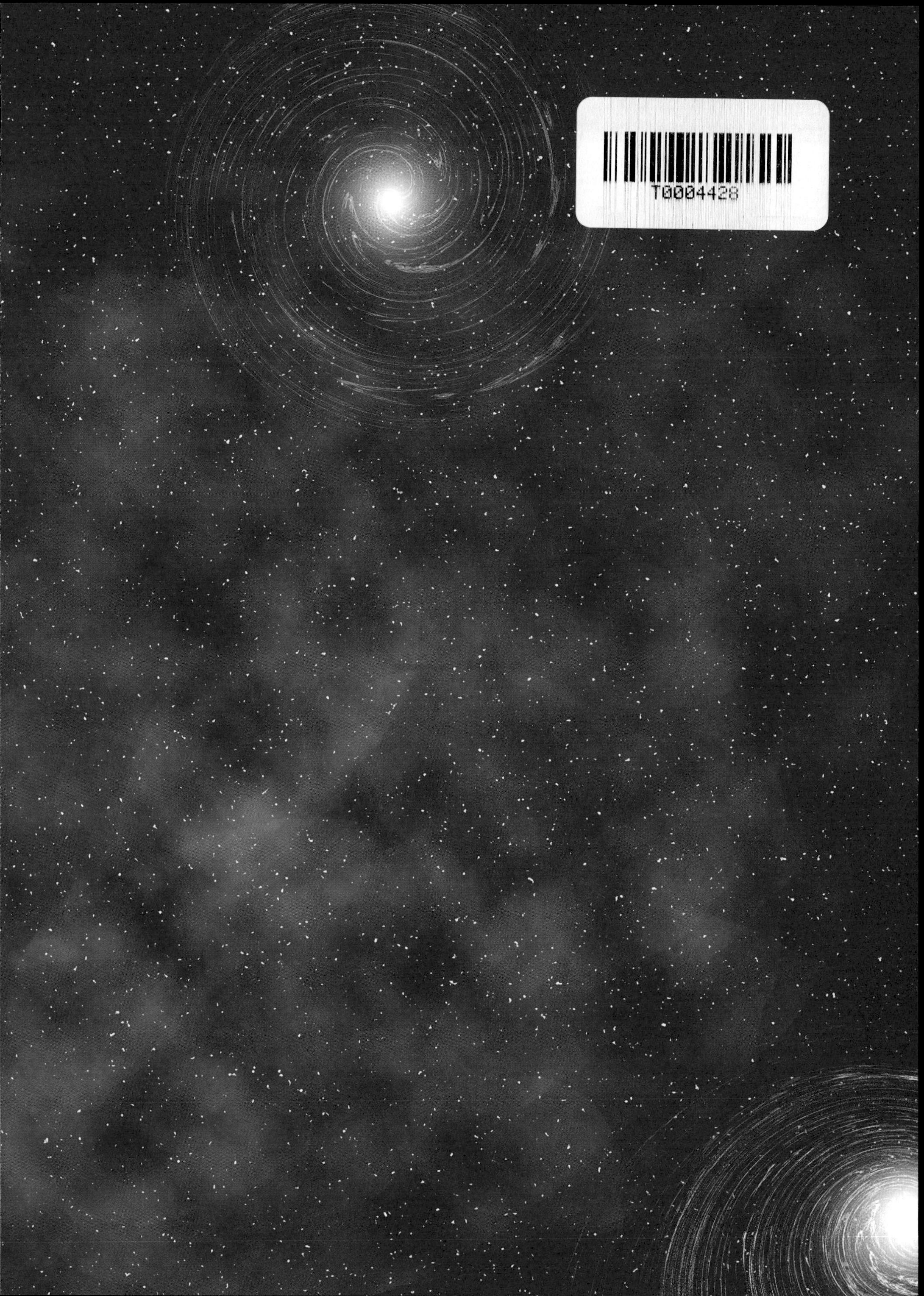

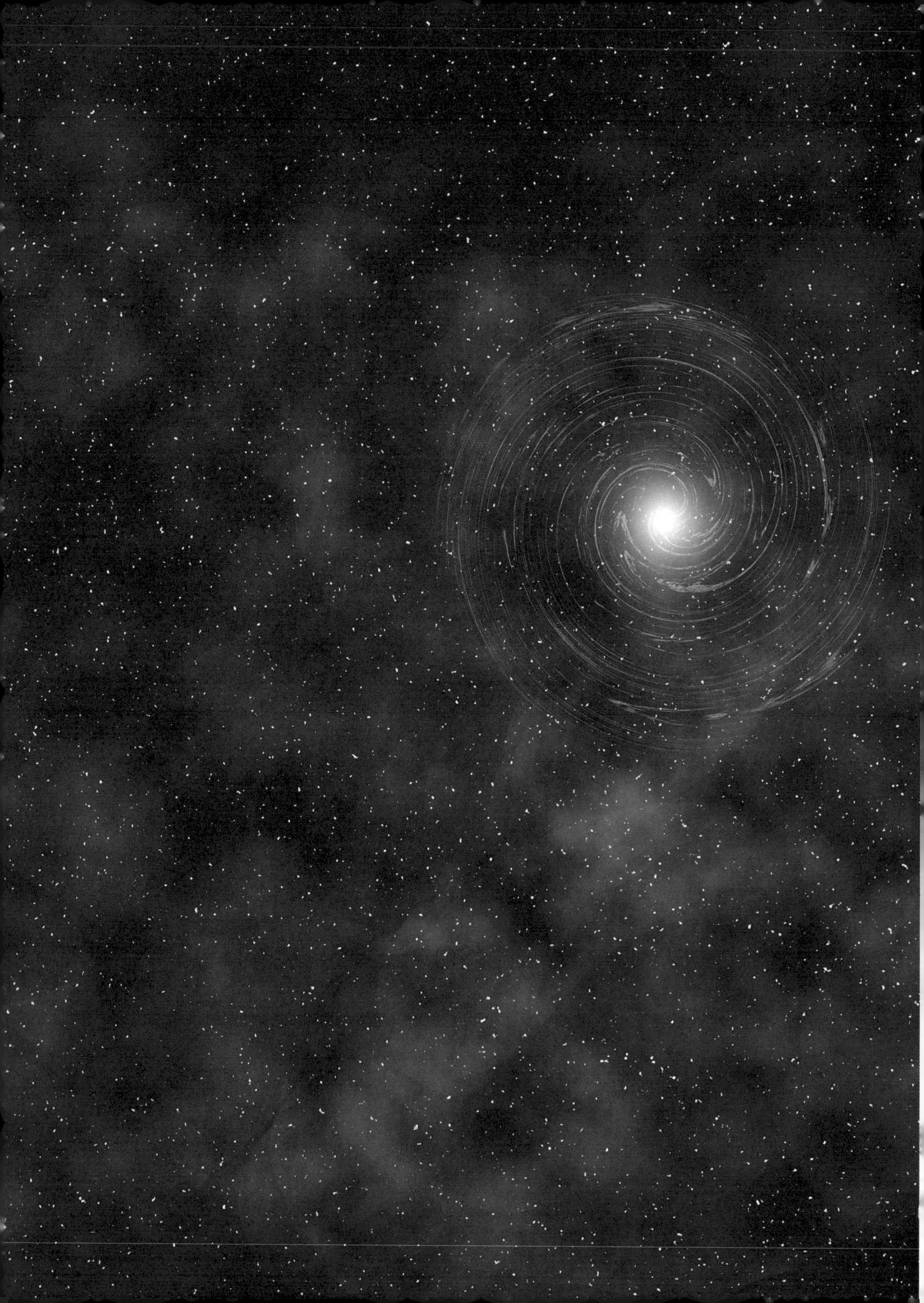

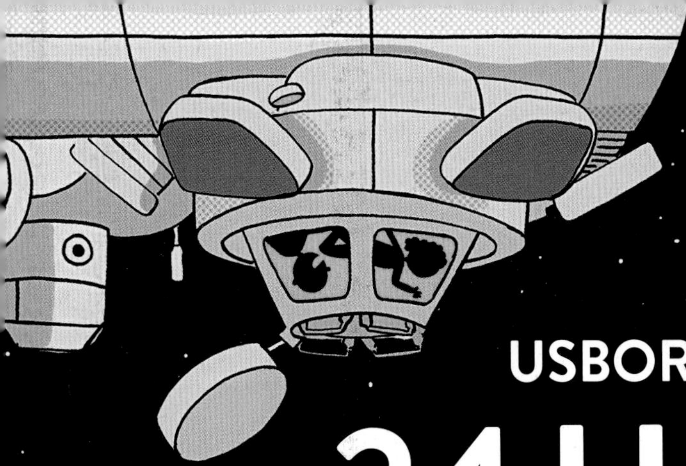

USBORNE

24 Hours in Space

Rob Lloyd Jones

Illustrated by Laurent Kling

Designed by Samantha Barrett

Consultants: Libby Jackson

Libby Jackson is is the Exploration Science Manager at the UK Space Agency.

Stuart Atkinson

Stuart Atkinson is an outreach educator and author of many books about astronomy and spaceflight.

Usborne Quicklinks

For links to websites and videos where you can find out more about what it's like for astronauts living in space, go to usborne.com/Quicklinks and type in the title of this book.

Here are some of the things you can do at the websites we recommend:

- Watch astronauts floating and exercising aboard the ISS.
- See how an astronaut eats his dessert in Zero-G.
- Explore the ISS with an astronaut.
- Take a fun quiz to see if you have what it takes to become an astronaut.
- Spot the ISS in the night sky from your home.

Please follow the online safety guidelines at Usborne Quicklinks. Children should be supervised online. Usborne Publishing is not responsible for the content of external websites.

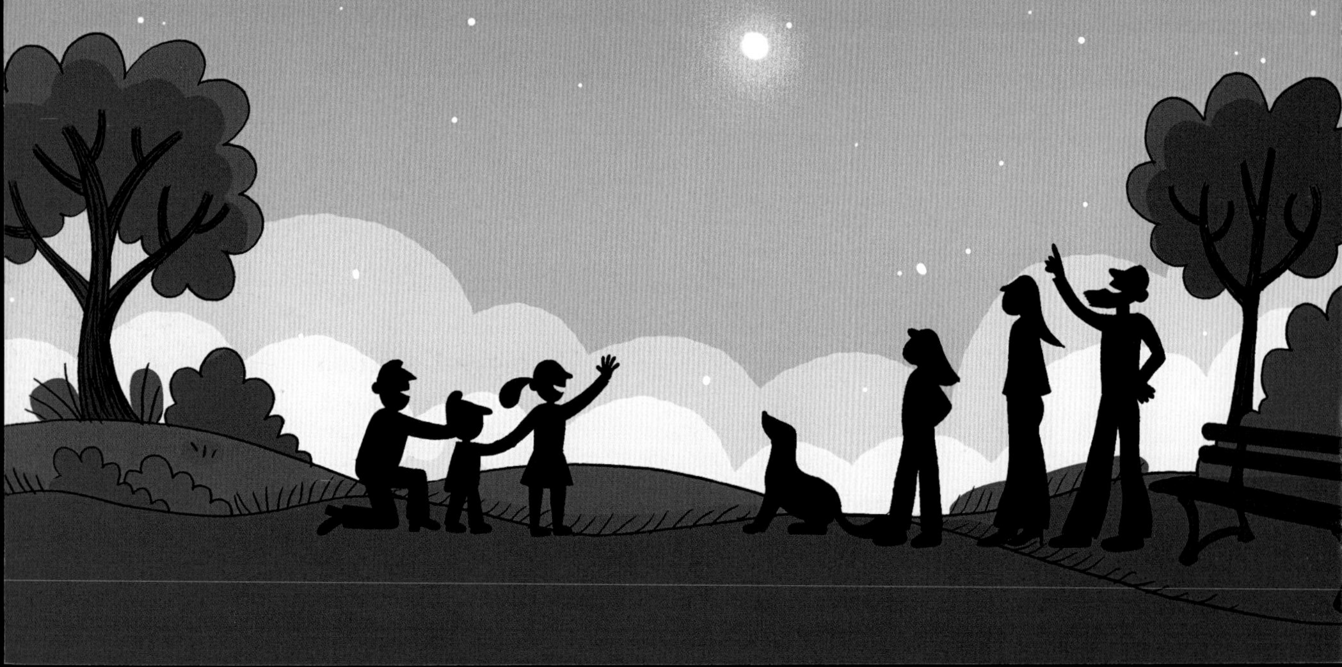

CONTENTS

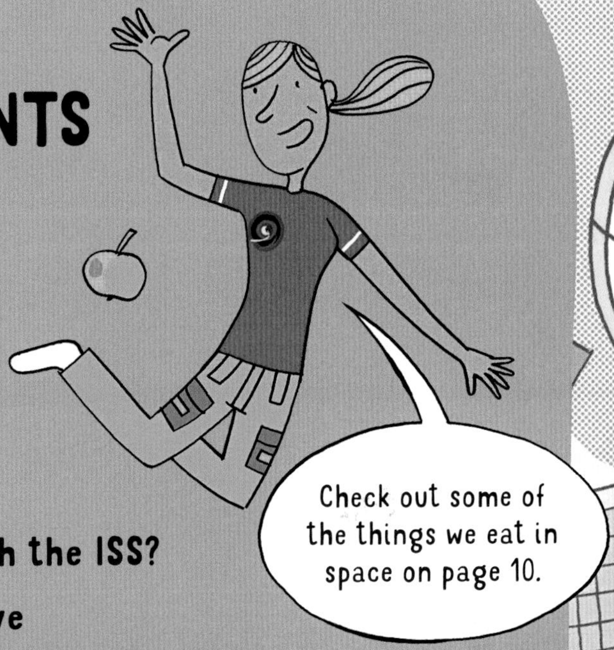

Check out some of the things we eat in space on page 10.

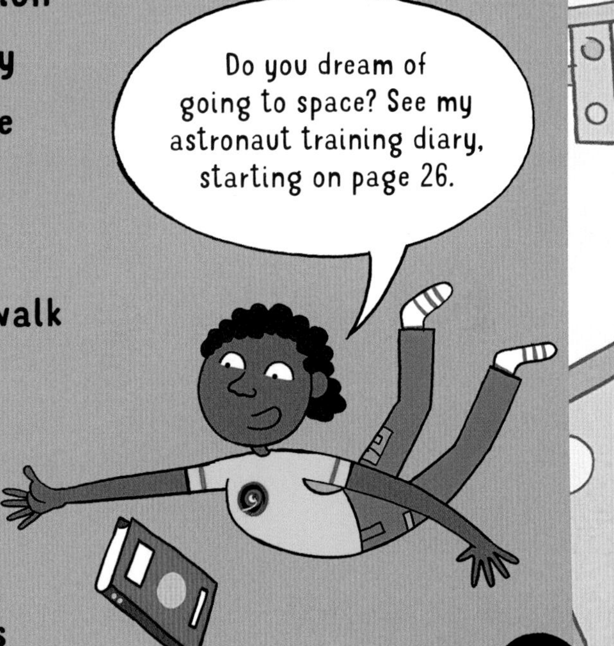

Do you dream of going to space? See my astronaut training diary, starting on page 26.

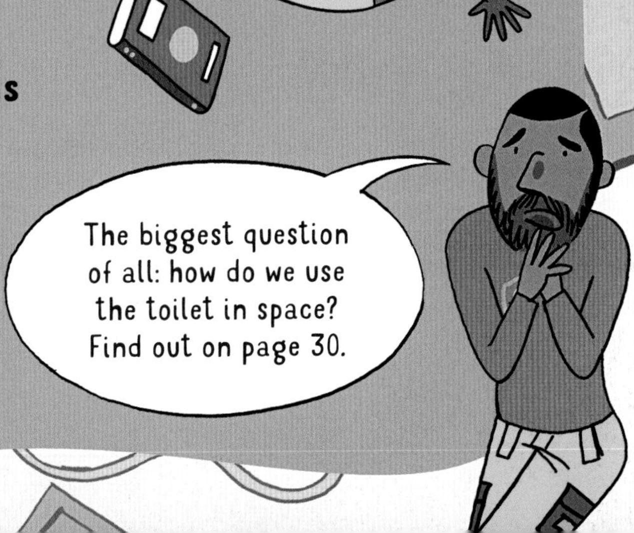

The biggest question of all: how do we use the toilet in space? Find out on page 30.

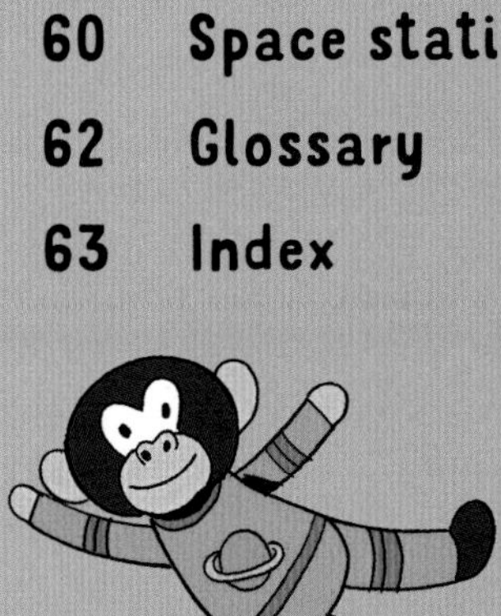

Outer space.
Far* above Earth.
The International Space Station drifts. All is calm. All is quiet...
...until a frantic cry rings out.
IT'S ESCAPED! Nooo!
It's loose!
I can catch it...
*Actually about 400km, or 250 miles.

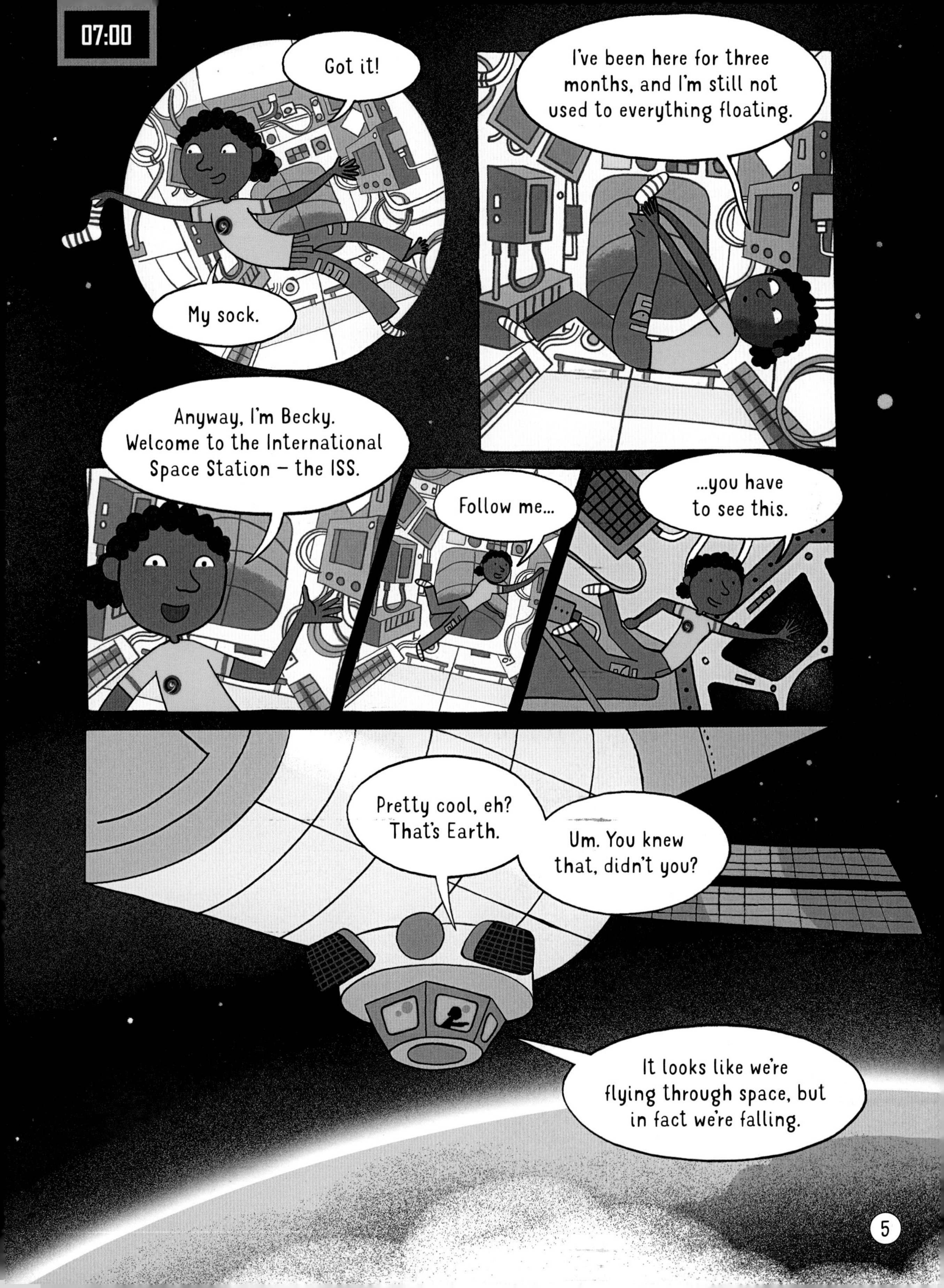
07:00
Got it!
My sock.
I've been here for three months, and I'm still not used to everything floating.
Anyway, I'm Becky. Welcome to the International Space Station – the ISS.
Follow me...
...you have to see this.
Pretty cool, eh? That's Earth.
Um. You knew that, didn't you?
It looks like we're flying through space, but in fact we're falling.

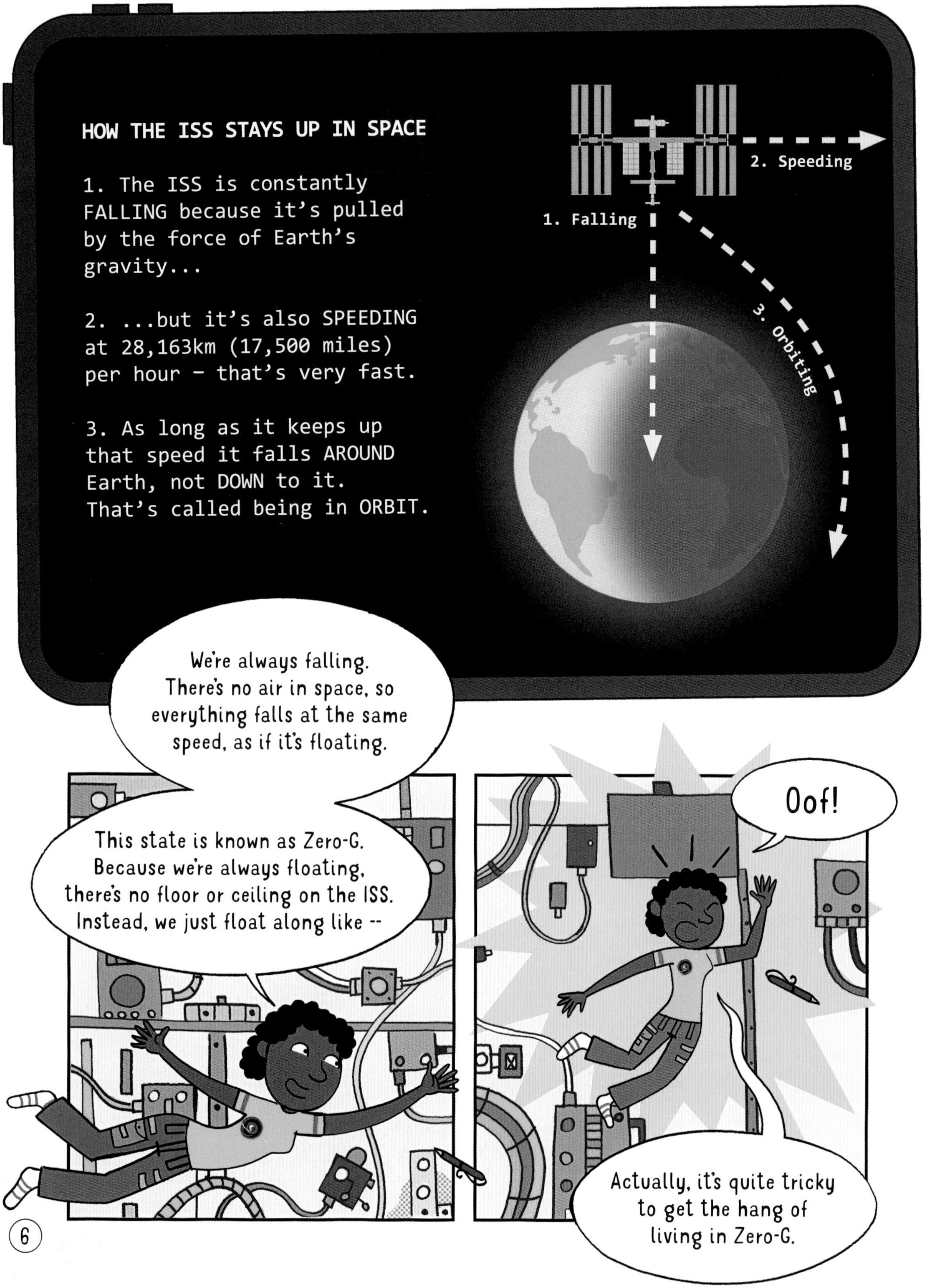
HOW THE ISS STAYS UP IN SPACE
1. The ISS is constantly FALLING because it's pulled by the force of Earth's gravity...
2. ...but it's also SPEEDING at 28,163km (17,500 miles) per hour – that's very fast.
3. As long as it keeps up that speed it falls AROUND Earth, not DOWN to it. That's called being in ORBIT.
1. Falling
2. Speeding
3. Orbiting
We're always falling. There's no air in space, so everything falls at the same speed, as if it's floating.
This state is known as Zero-G. Because we're always floating, there's no floor or ceiling on the ISS. Instead, we just float along like --
Oof!
Actually, it's quite tricky to get the hang of living in Zero-G.

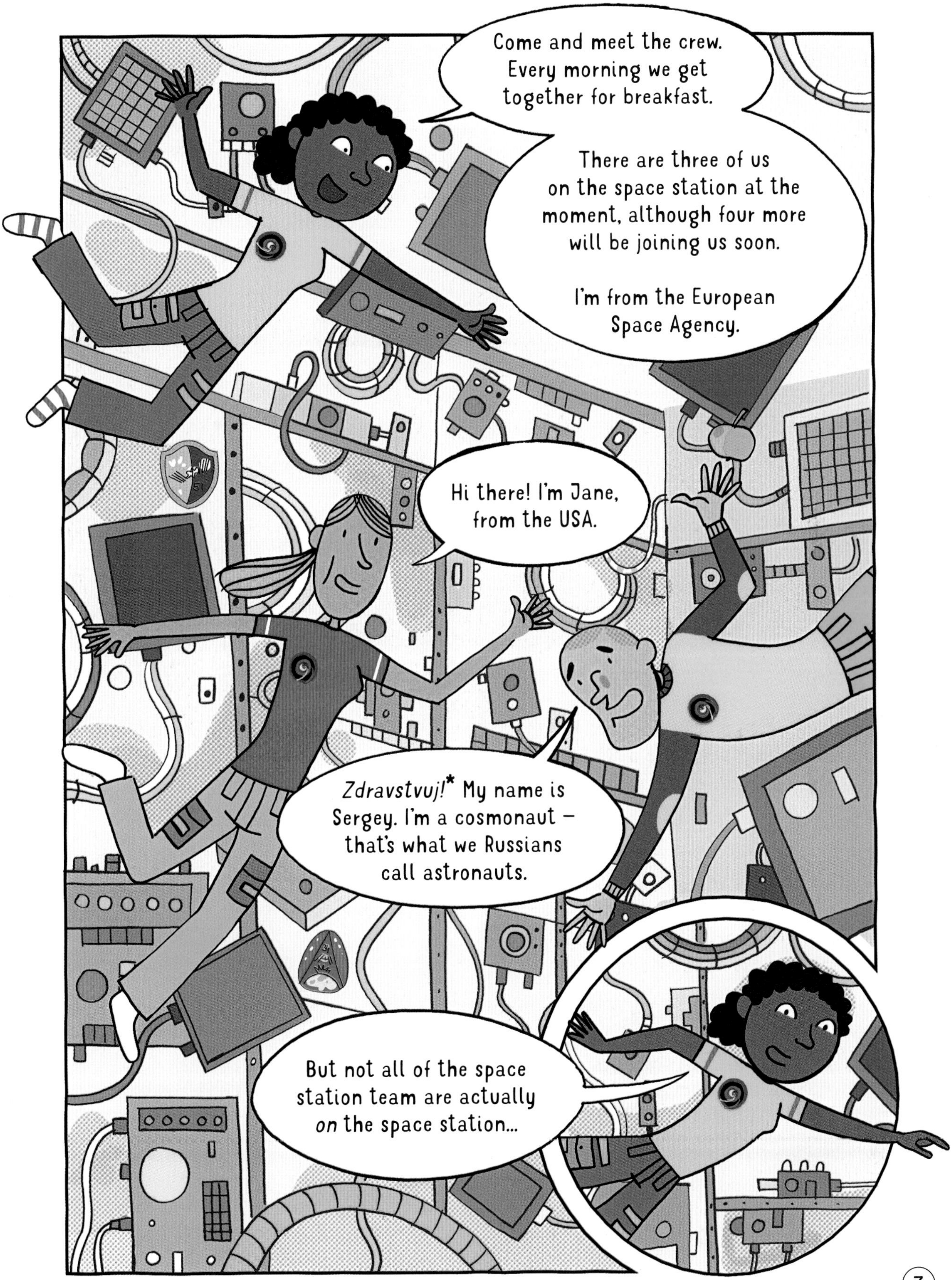
Come and meet the crew. Every morning we get together for breakfast.
There are three of us on the space station at the moment, although four more will be joining us soon.
I'm from the European Space Agency.
Hi there! I'm Jane, from the USA.
*Zdravstvuj!** My name is Sergey. I'm a cosmonaut – that's what we Russians call astronauts.
But not all of the space station team are actually *on* the space station...

* "Hello," in Russian

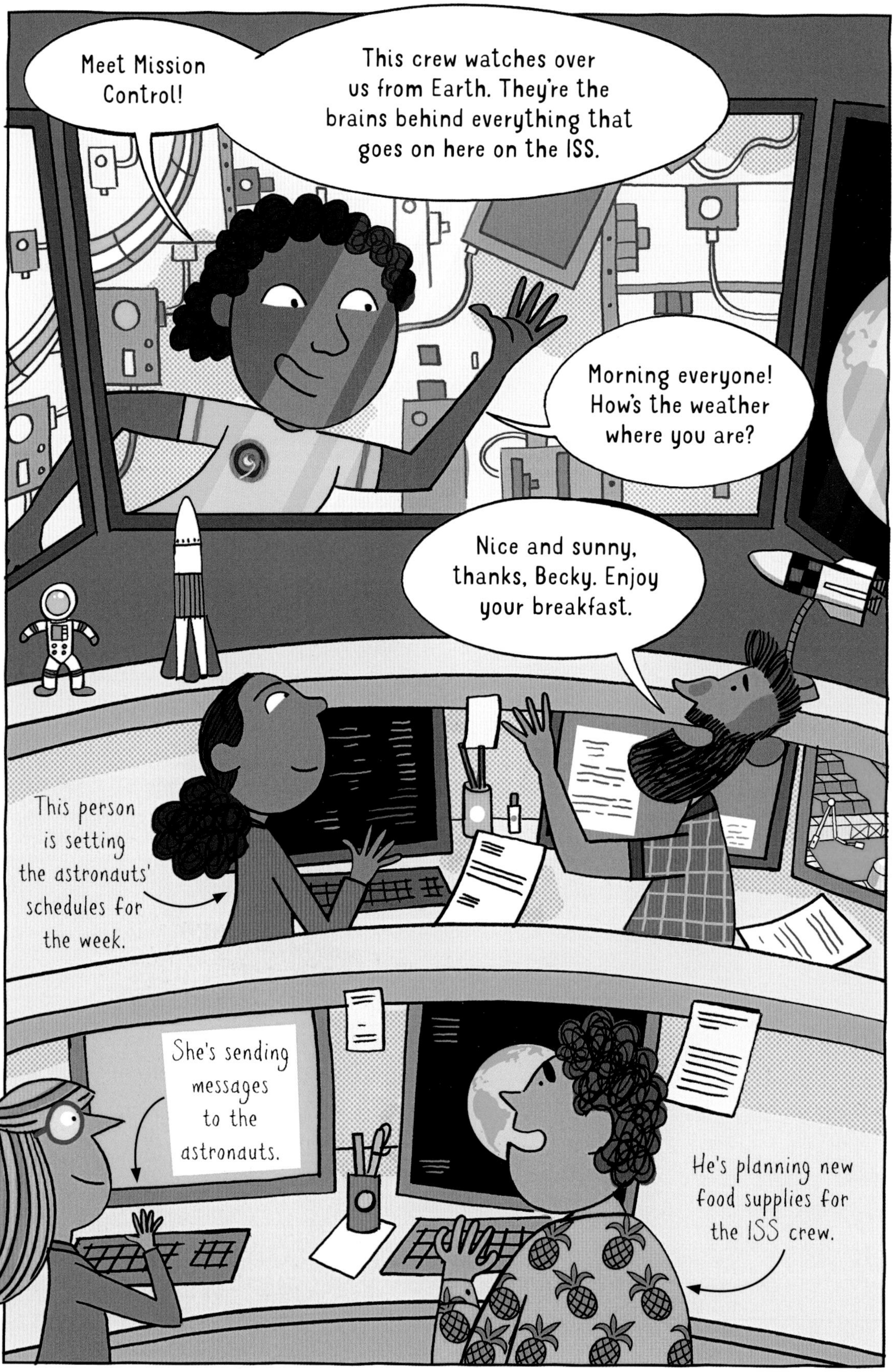

Meet Mission Control!
This crew watches over us from Earth. They're the brains behind everything that goes on here on the ISS.
Morning everyone! How's the weather where you are?
Nice and sunny, thanks, Becky. Enjoy your breakfast.
This person is setting the astronauts' schedules for the week.
She's sending messages to the astronauts.
He's planning new food supplies for the ISS crew.

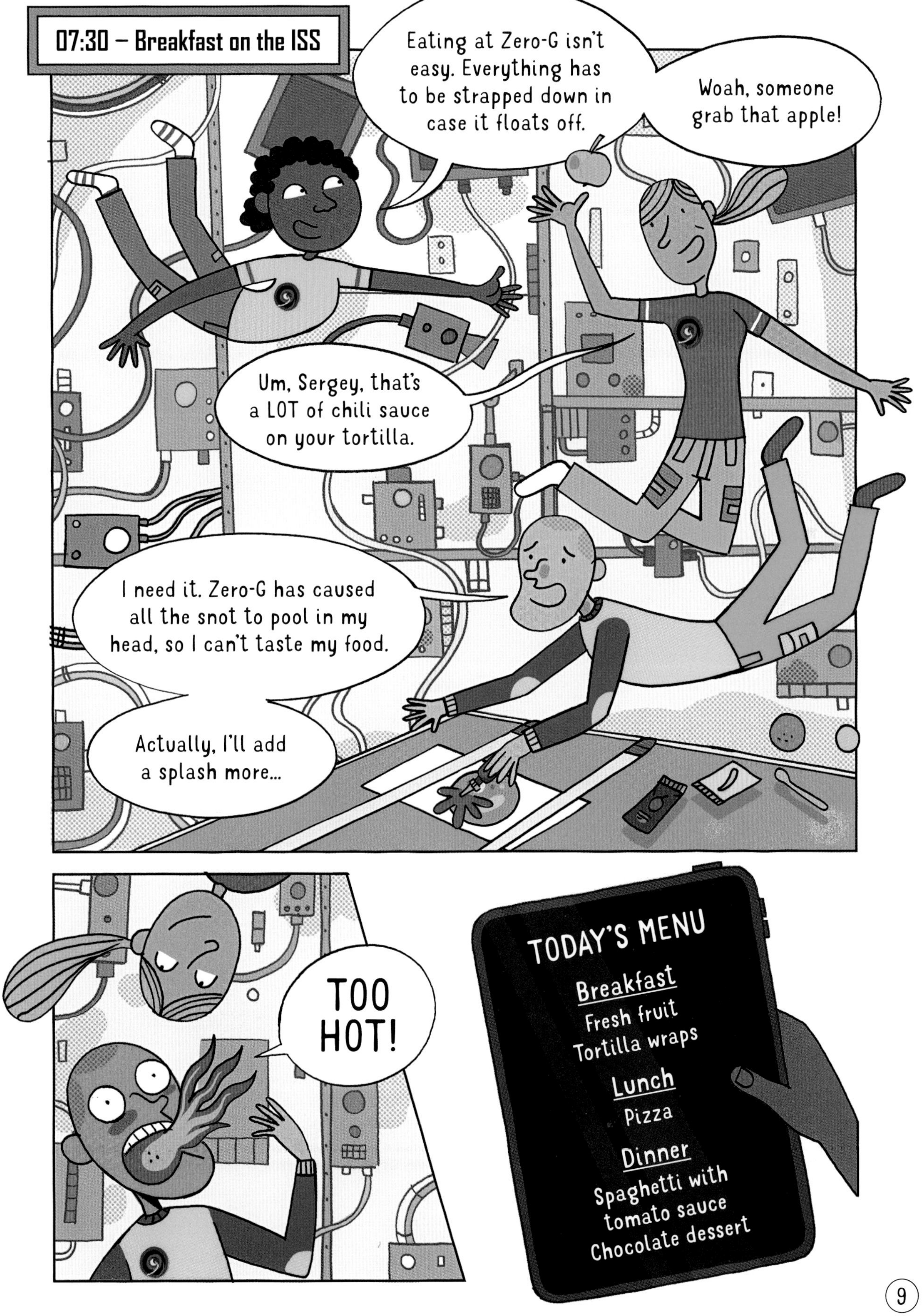
07:30 – Breakfast on the ISS
Eating at Zero-G isn't easy. Everything has to be strapped down in case it floats off.
Woah, someone grab that apple!
Um, Sergey, that's a LOT of chili sauce on your tortilla.
I need it. Zero-G has caused all the snot to pool in my head, so I can't taste my food.
Actually, I'll add a splash more...
TOO HOT!
TODAY'S MENU
Breakfast
Fresh fruit
Tortilla wraps
Lunch
Pizza
Dinner
Spaghetti with tomato sauce
Chocolate dessert

Space food

Before each mission, astronauts choose what they want to eat on the ISS. This food is specially prepared to last several months, and designed to avoid crumbs that might float off and damage the station's controls.

Dried food

Just add water and these are ready to eat.

Pre-cooked meals

Simply warm these in an oven.

Fresh food

Supplies of fresh fruit and vegetables are eaten quickly, before they rot, so they don't usually last very long.

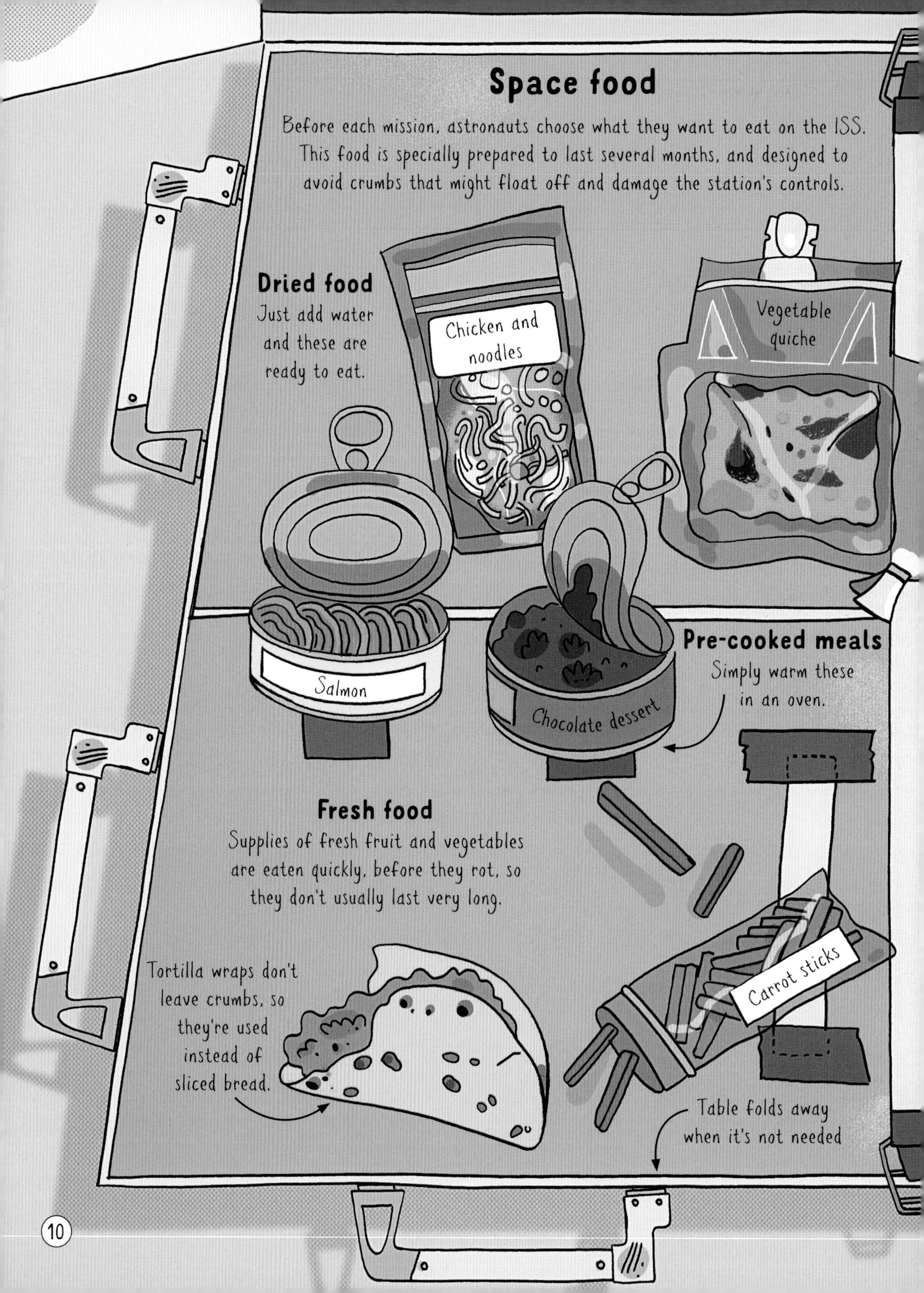

Chicken and noodles
Vegetable quiche
Salmon
Chocolate dessert
Carrot sticks
Tortilla wraps don't leave crumbs, so they're used instead of sliced bread.
Table folds away when it's not needed

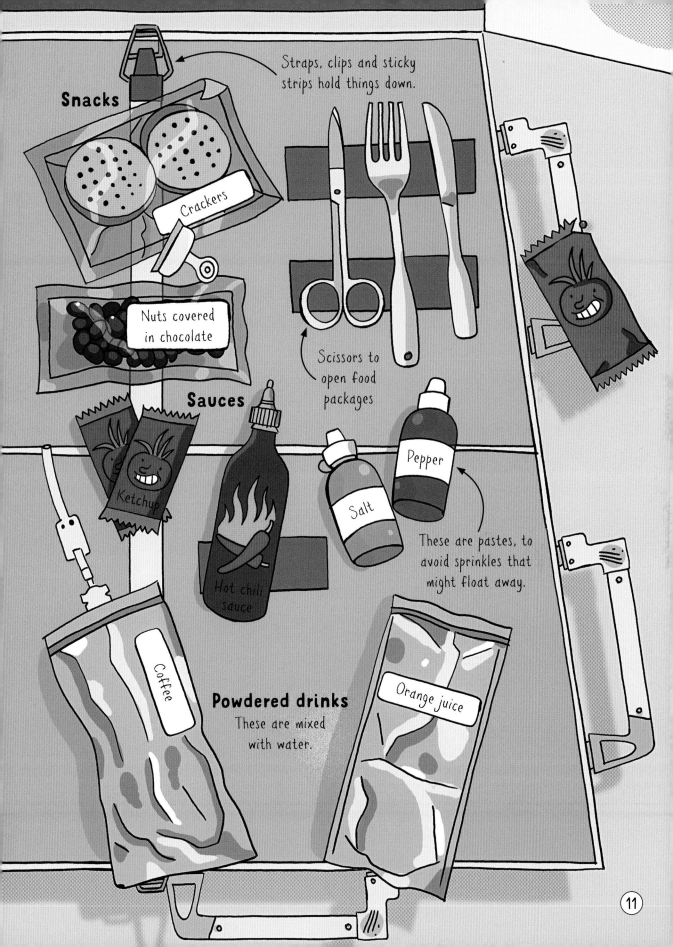

Snacks

Straps, clips and sticky strips hold things down.

Crackers

Nuts covered in chocolate

Scissors to open food packages

Sauces

Ketchup

Hot chili sauce

Salt

Pepper

These are pastes, to avoid sprinkles that might float away.

Coffee

Powdered drinks
These are mixed with water.

Orange juice

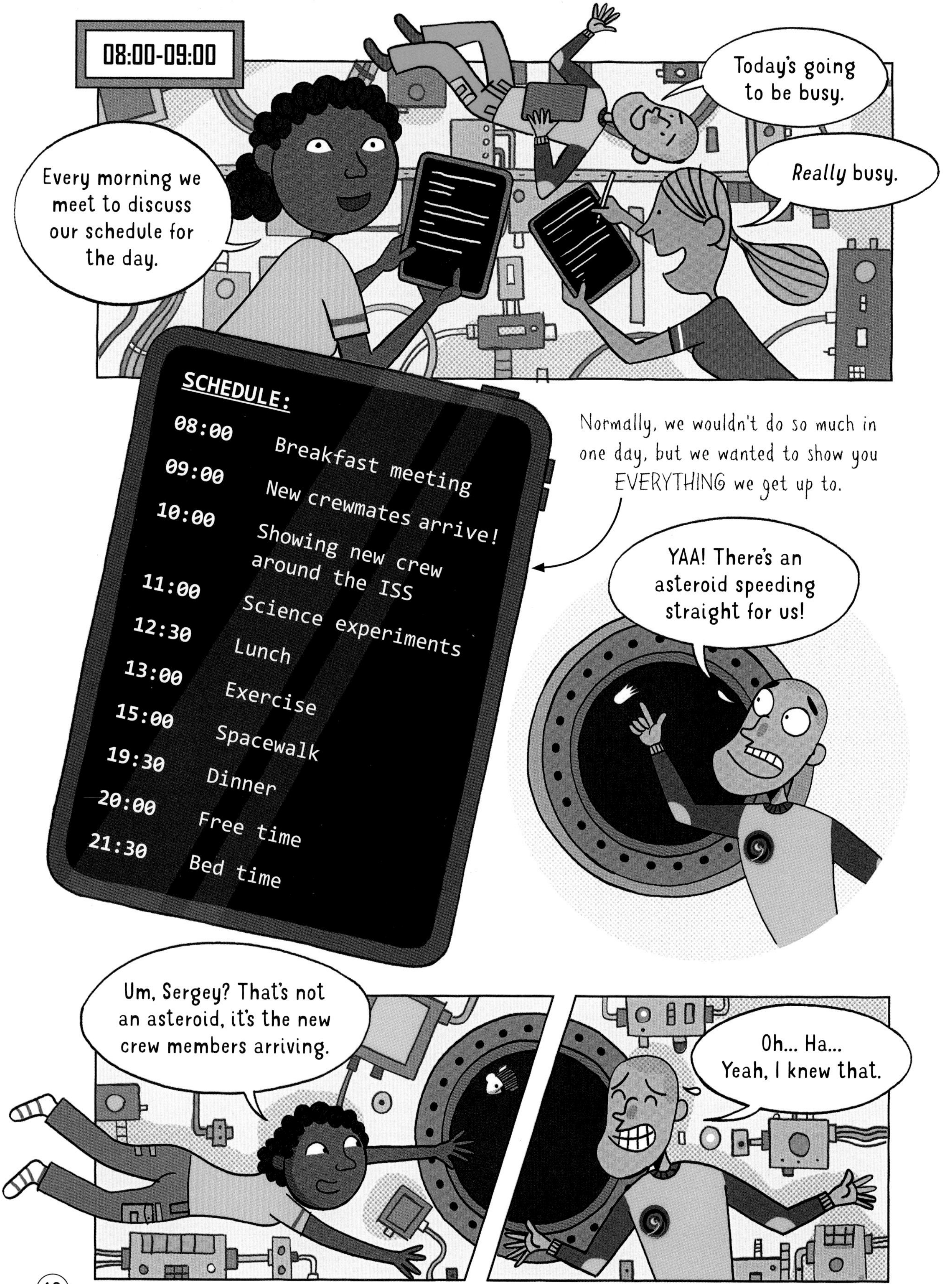
08:00-09:00
Every morning we meet to discuss our schedule for the day.
Today's going to be busy.
Really busy.
SCHEDULE:
08:00 Breakfast meeting
09:00 New crewmates arrive!
10:00 Showing new crew around the ISS
11:00 Science experiments
12:30 Lunch
13:00 Exercise
15:00 Spacewalk
19:30 Dinner
20:00 Free time
21:30 Bed time
Normally, we wouldn't do so much in one day, but we wanted to show you EVERYTHING we get up to.
YAA! There's an asteroid speeding straight for us!
Um, Sergey? That's not an asteroid, it's the new crew members arriving.
Oh... Ha... Yeah, I knew that.

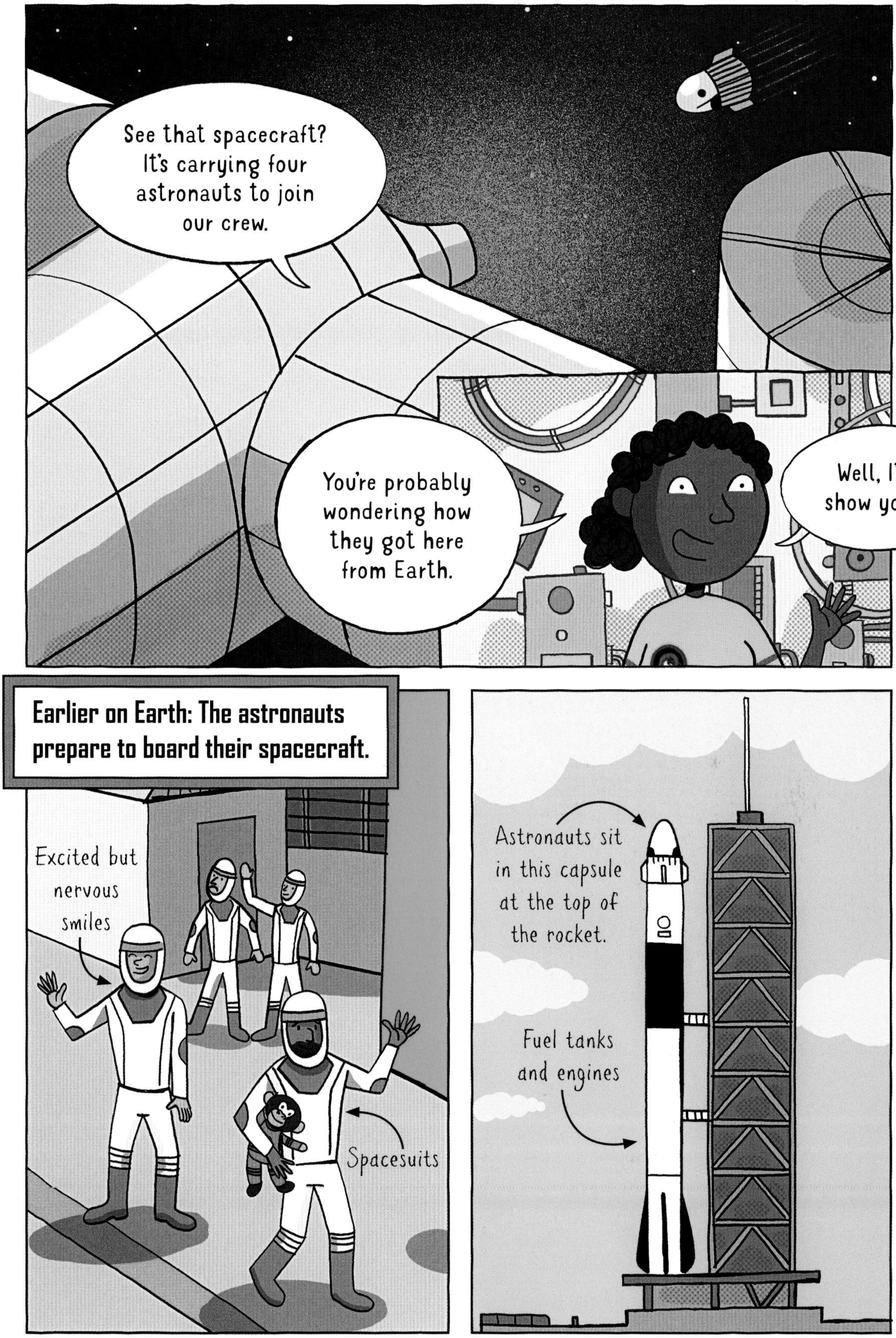
See that spacecraft? It's carrying four astronauts to join our crew.
You're probably wondering how they got here from Earth.
Well, I'll show you...
Earlier on Earth: The astronauts prepare to board their spacecraft.
Excited but nervous smiles
Spacesuits
Astronauts sit in this capsule at the top of the rocket.
Fuel tanks and engines

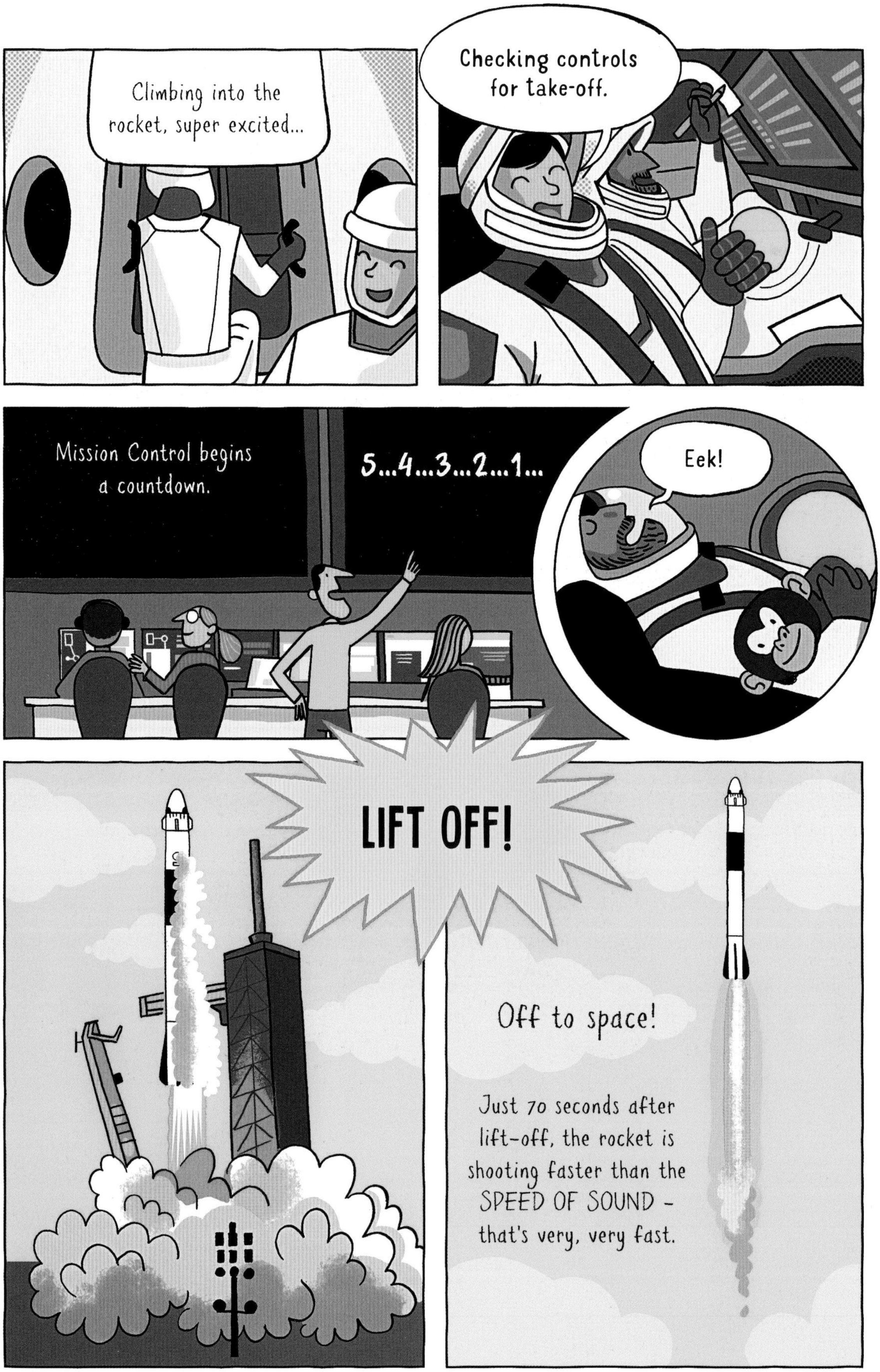

Climbing into the rocket, super excited...
Checking controls for take-off.
Mission Control begins a countdown.
5...4...3...2...1...
Eek!
LIFT OFF!
Off to space!
Just 70 seconds after lift-off, the rocket is shooting faster than the SPEED OF SOUND – that's very, very fast.

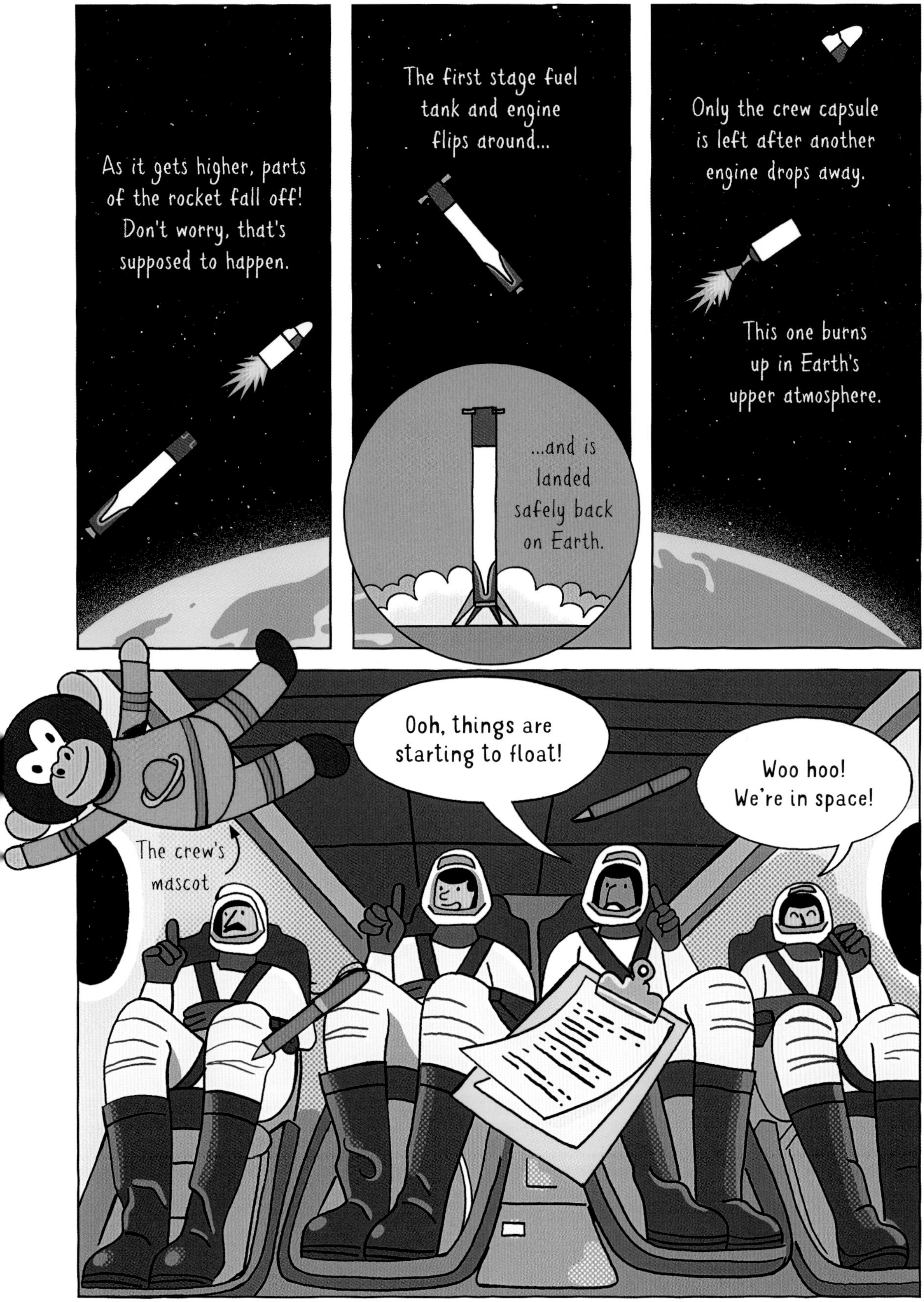
As it gets higher, parts of the rocket fall off! Don't worry, that's supposed to happen.
The first stage fuel tank and engine flips around...
...and is landed safely back on Earth.
Only the crew capsule is left after another engine drops away.
This one burns up in Earth's upper atmosphere.
The crew's mascot
Ooh, things are starting to float!
Woo hoo! We're in space!

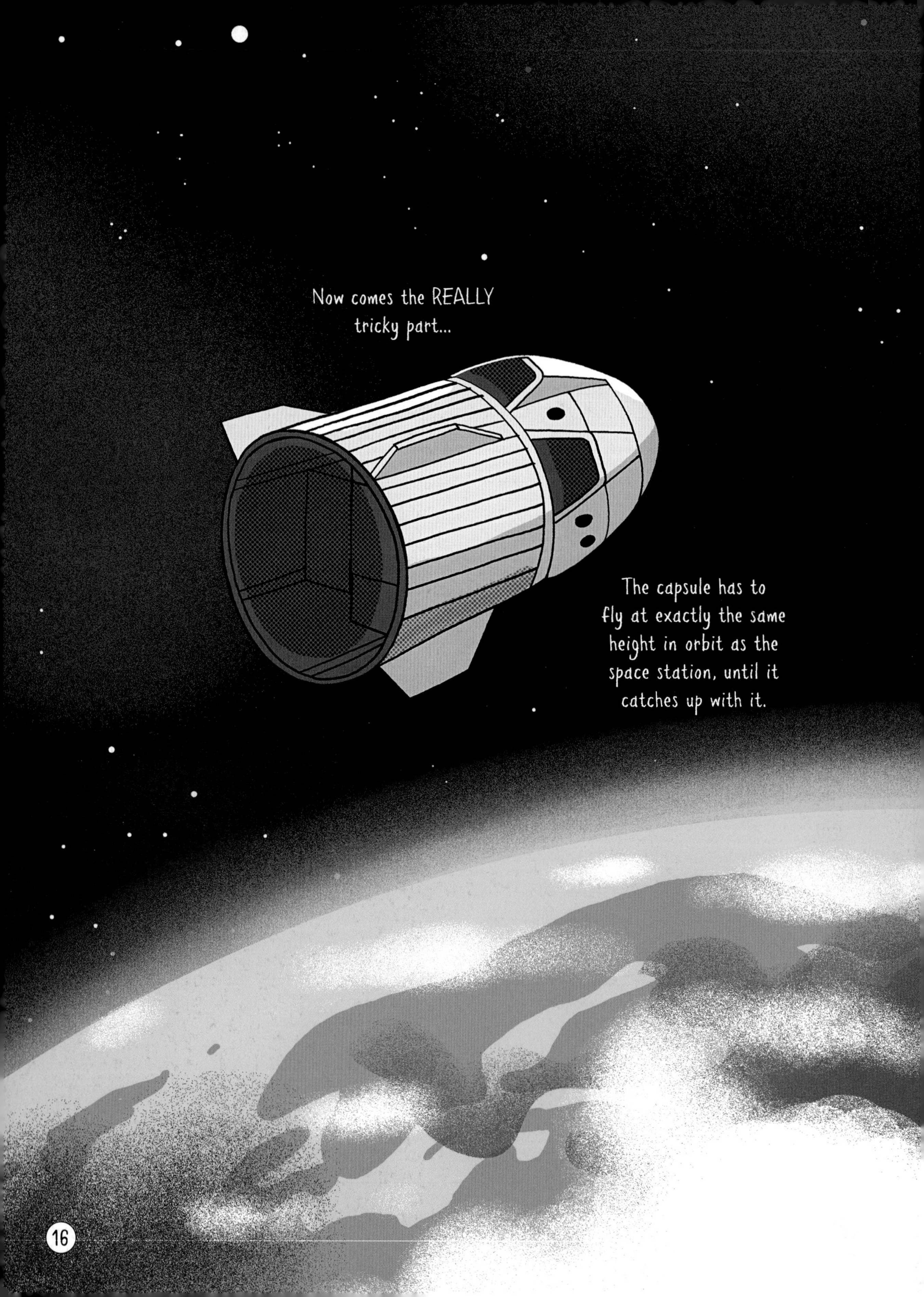
Now comes the REALLY tricky part...
The capsule has to fly at exactly the same height in orbit as the space station, until it catches up with it.

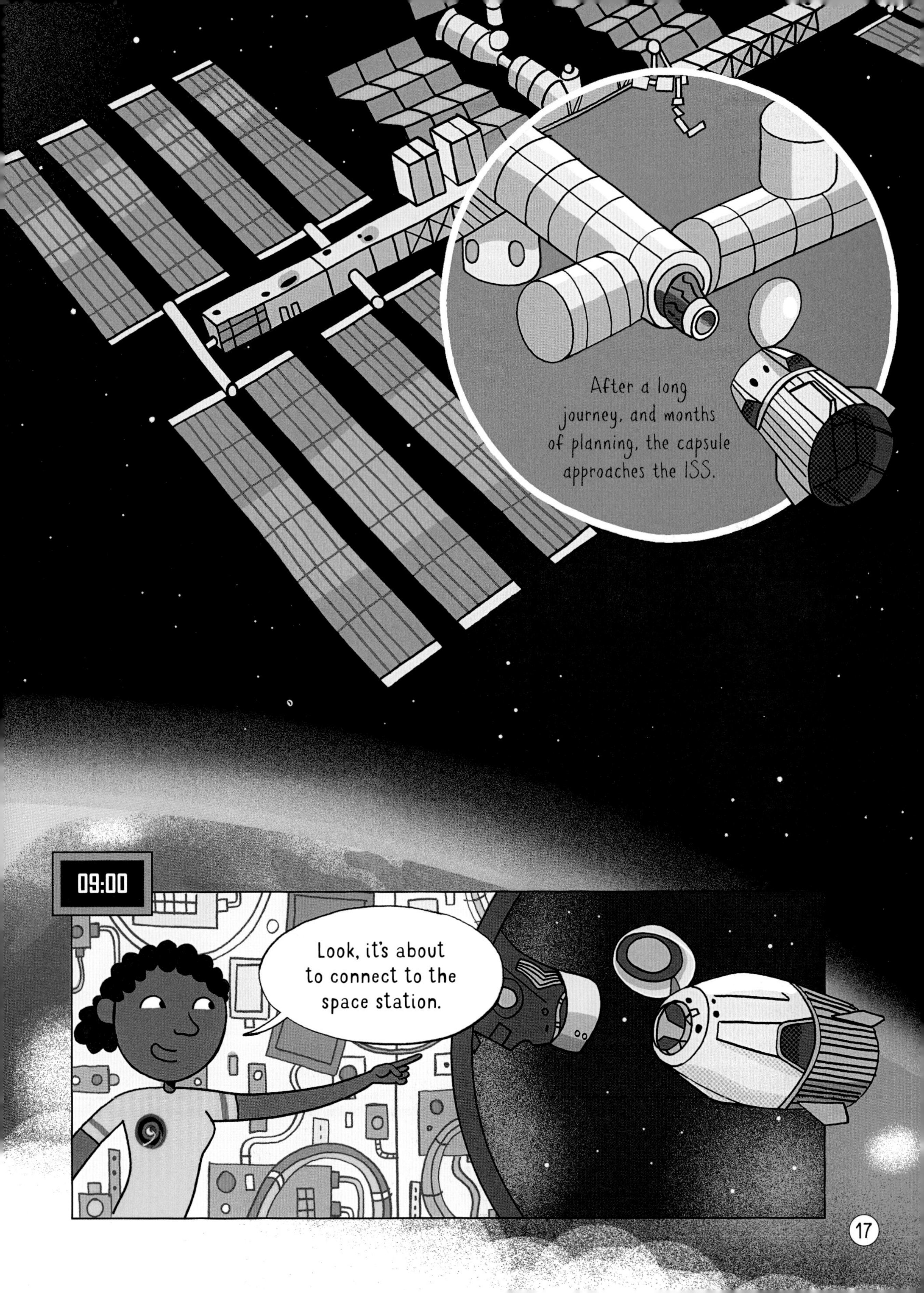
After a long journey, and months of planning, the capsule approaches the ISS.
09:00
Look, it's about to connect to the space station.

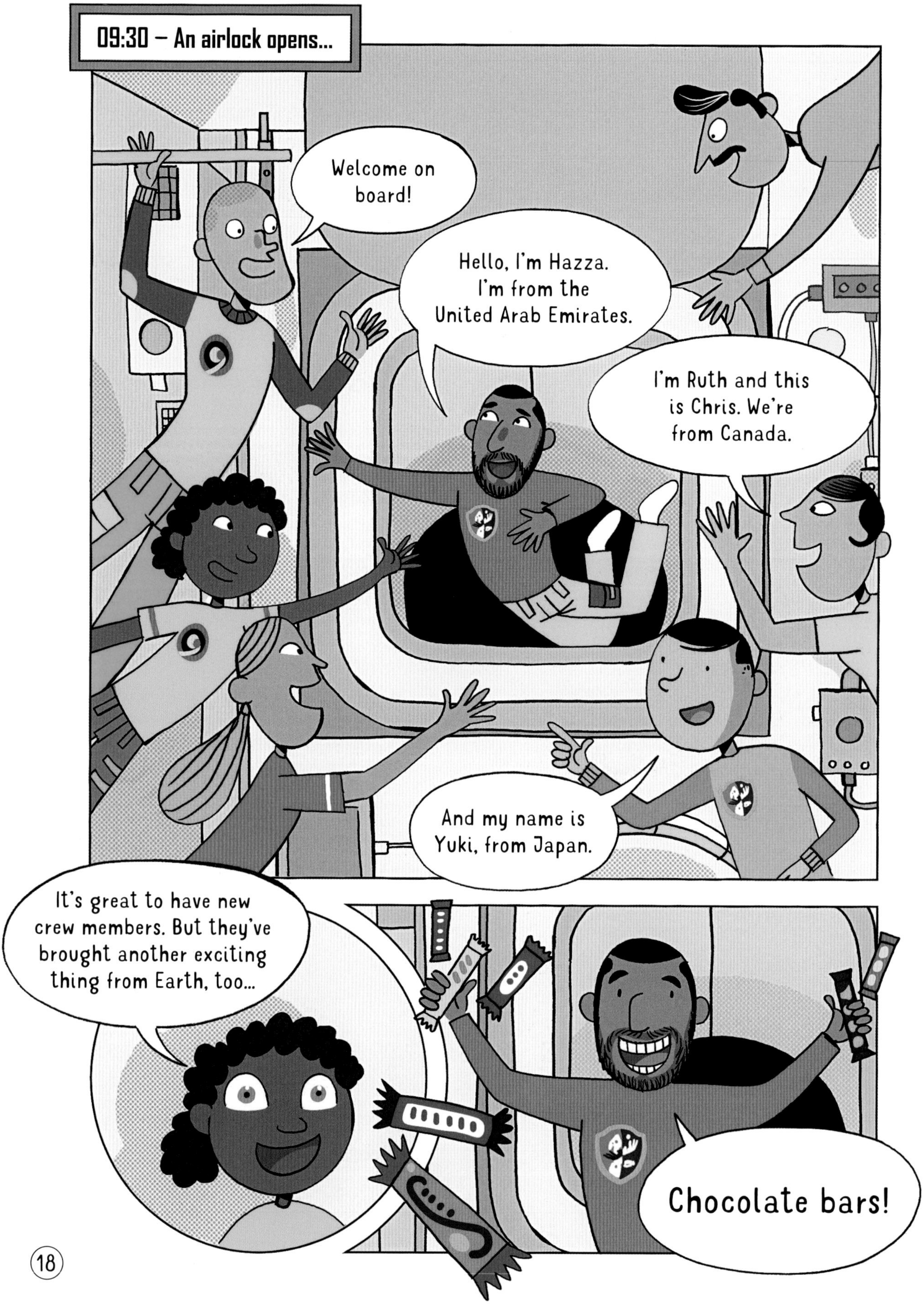

09:30 – An airlock opens...
Welcome on board!
Hello, I'm Hazza. I'm from the United Arab Emirates.
I'm Ruth and this is Chris. We're from Canada.
And my name is Yuki, from Japan.
It's great to have new crew members. But they've brought another exciting thing from Earth, too...
Chocolate bars!

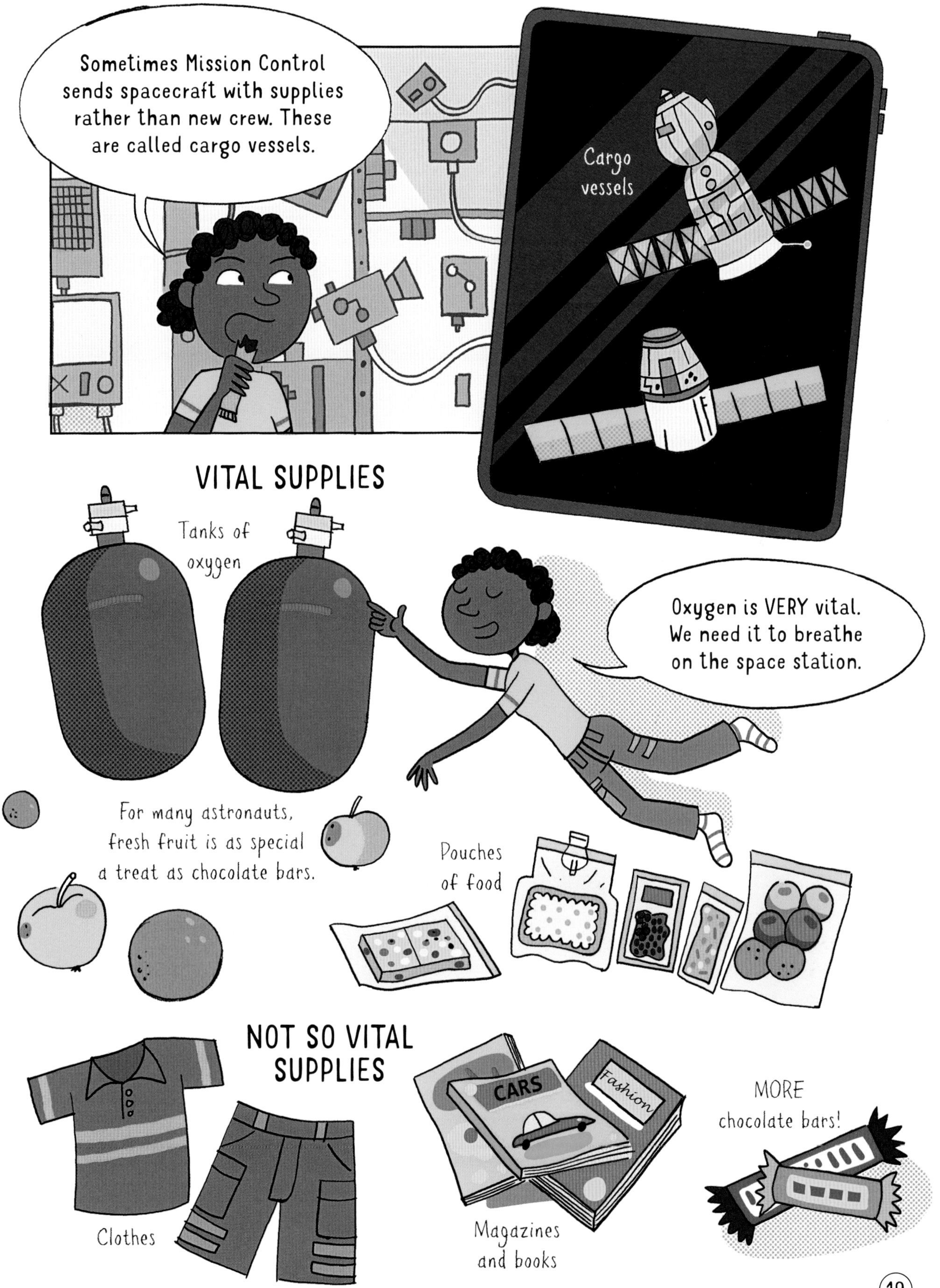

Sometimes Mission Control sends spacecraft with supplies rather than new crew. These are called cargo vessels.
Cargo vessels
VITAL SUPPLIES
Tanks of oxygen
Oxygen is VERY vital. We need it to breathe on the space station.
For many astronauts, fresh fruit is as special a treat as chocolate bars.
Pouches of food
NOT SO VITAL SUPPLIES
Clothes
CARS
Fashion
Magazines and books
MORE chocolate bars!

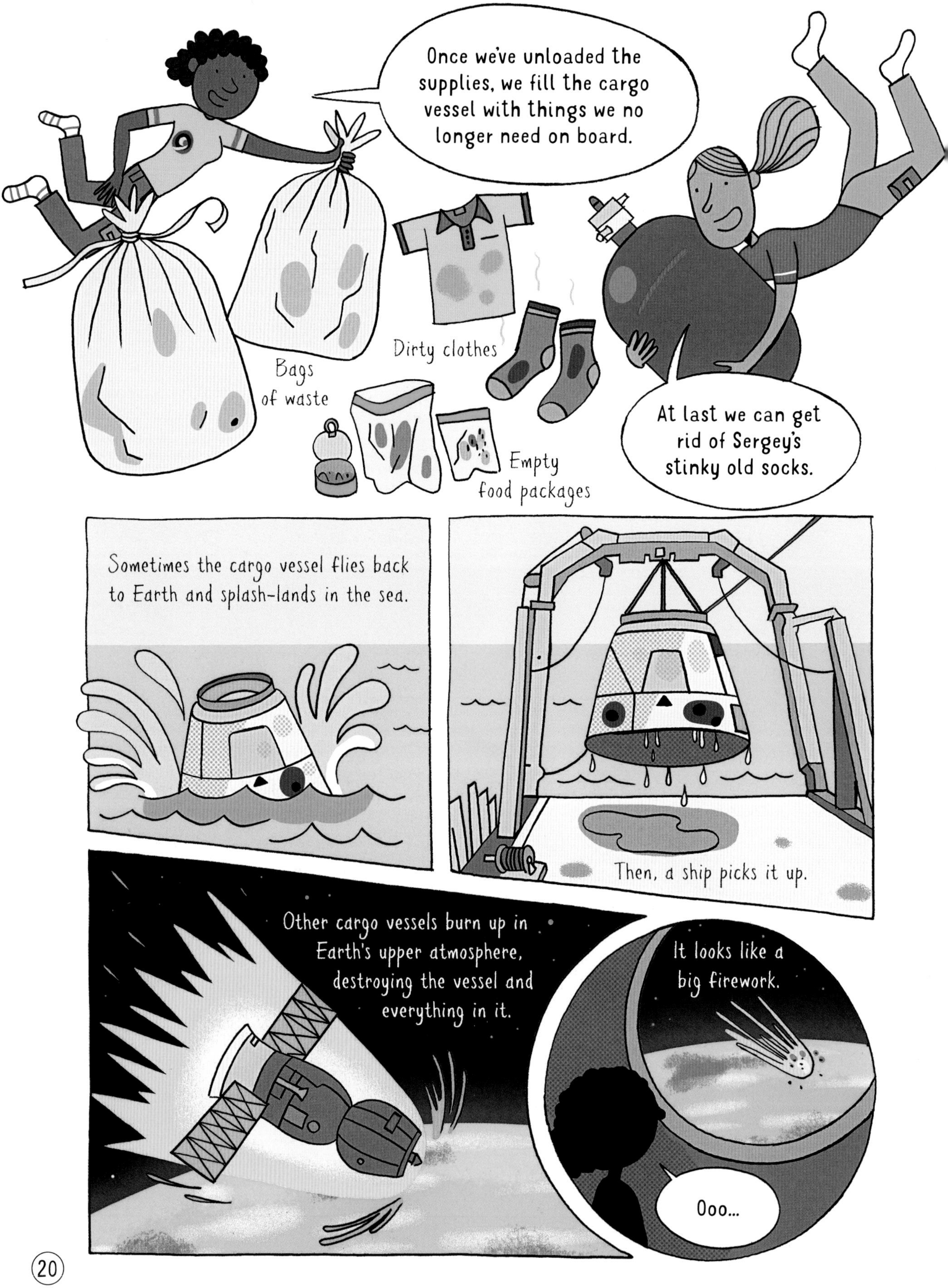
Once we've unloaded the supplies, we fill the cargo vessel with things we no longer need on board.
Bags of waste
Dirty clothes
Empty food packages
At last we can get rid of Sergey's stinky old socks.
Sometimes the cargo vessel flies back to Earth and splash-lands in the sea.
Then, a ship picks it up.
Other cargo vessels burn up in Earth's upper atmosphere, destroying the vessel and everything in it.
It looks like a big firework.
Ooo...

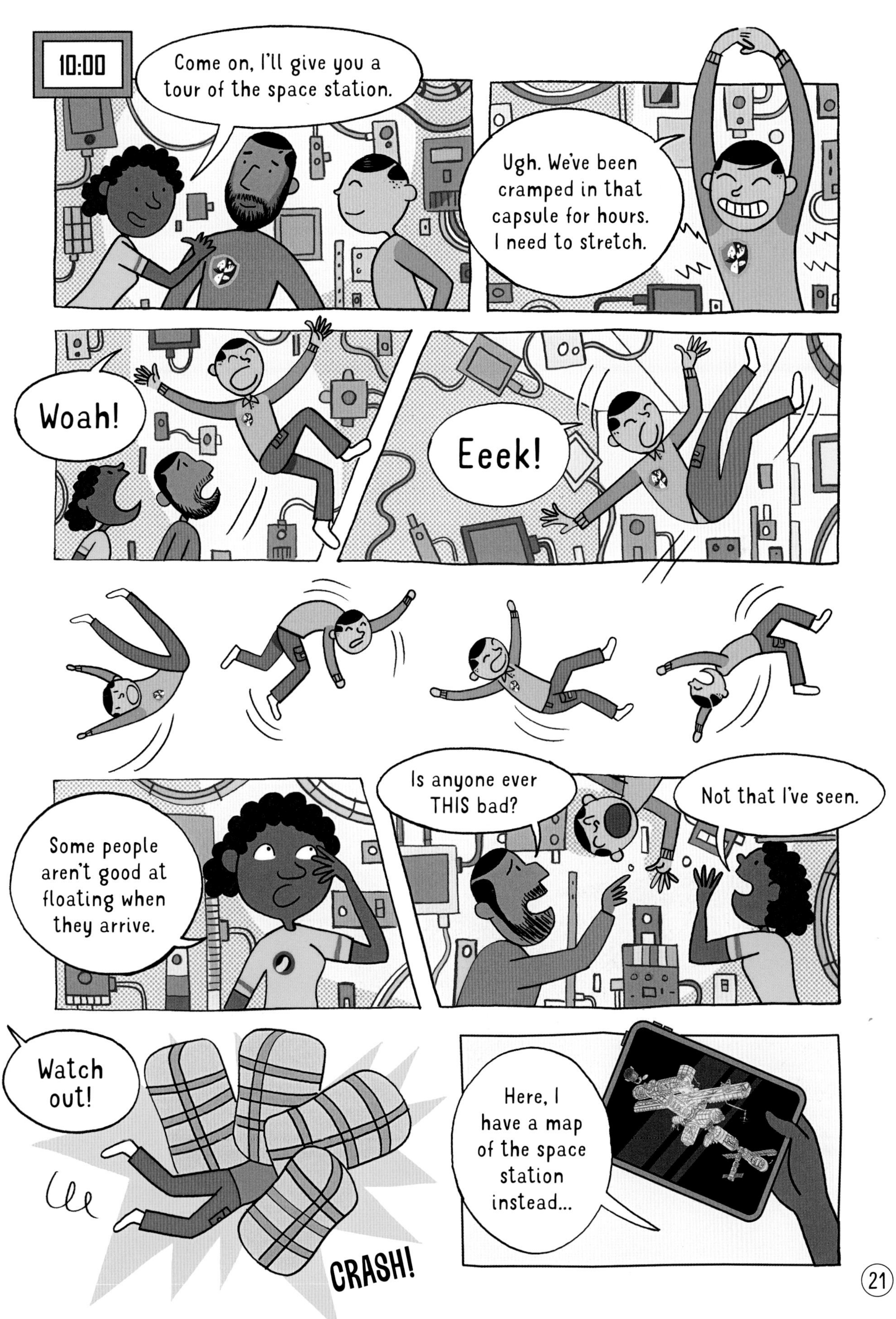
10:00
Come on, I'll give you a tour of the space station.
Ugh. We've been cramped in that capsule for hours. I need to stretch.
Woah!
Eeek!
Some people aren't good at floating when they arrive.
Is anyone ever THIS bad?
Not that I've seen.
Watch out!
CRASH!
Here, I have a map of the space station instead...

LOOKING AROUND THE ISS

The ISS is made up of lots of big parts called modules, which are linked together by little parts called nodes.

(Some of the modules in this diagram have been cut away so you can see inside.)

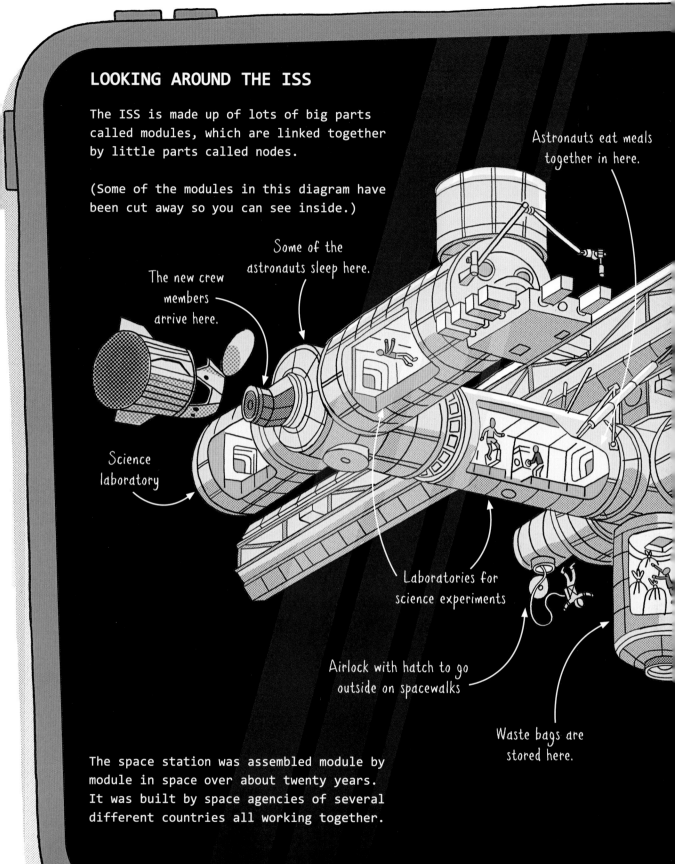

Astronauts eat meals together in here.

Some of the astronauts sleep here.

The new crew members arrive here.

Science laboratory

Laboratories for science experiments

Airlock with hatch to go outside on spacewalks

Waste bags are stored here.

The space station was assembled module by module in space over about twenty years. It was built by space agencies of several different countries all working together.

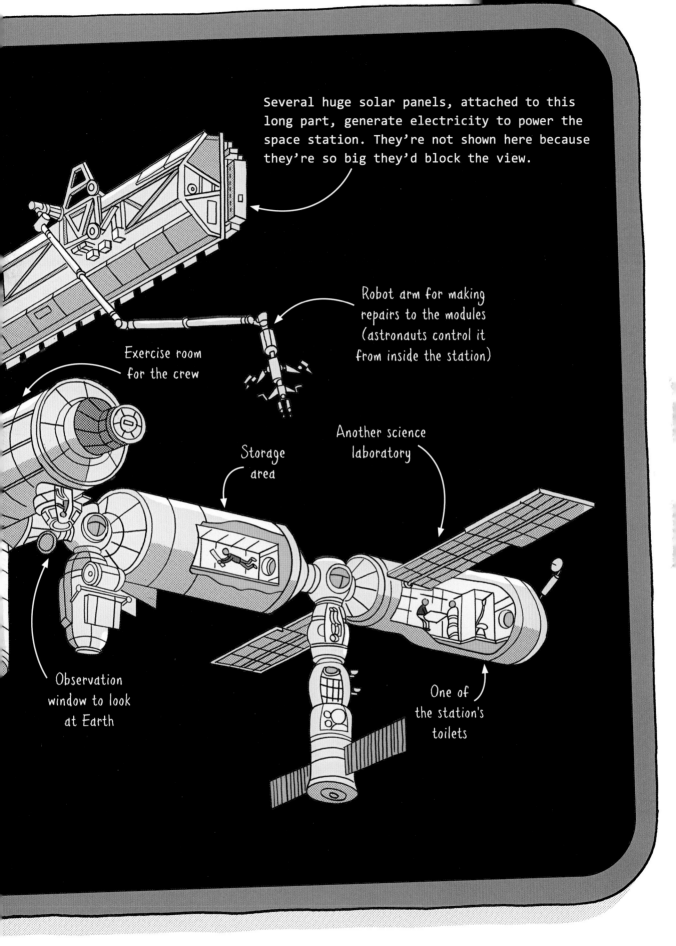

Several huge solar panels, attached to this long part, generate electricity to power the space station. They're not shown here because they're so big they'd block the view.

Robot arm for making repairs to the modules (astronauts control it from inside the station)

Exercise room for the crew

Storage area

Another science laboratory

Observation window to look at Earth

One of the station's toilets

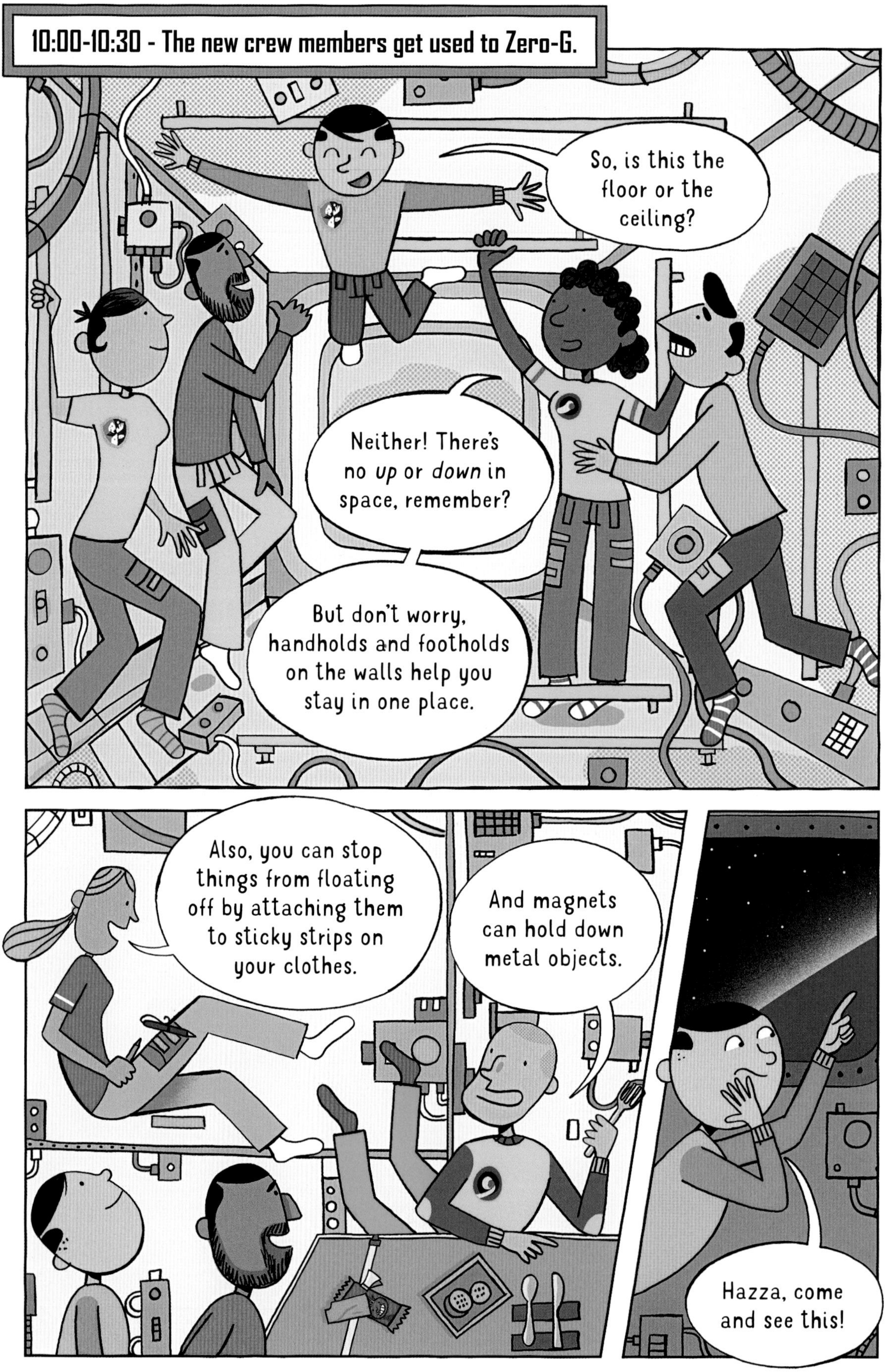
10:00-10:30 - The new crew members get used to Zero-G.
So, is this the floor or the ceiling?
Neither! There's no *up* or *down* in space, remember?
But don't worry, handholds and footholds on the walls help you stay in one place.
Also, you can stop things from floating off by attaching them to sticky strips on your clothes.
And magnets can hold down metal objects.
Hazza, come and see this!

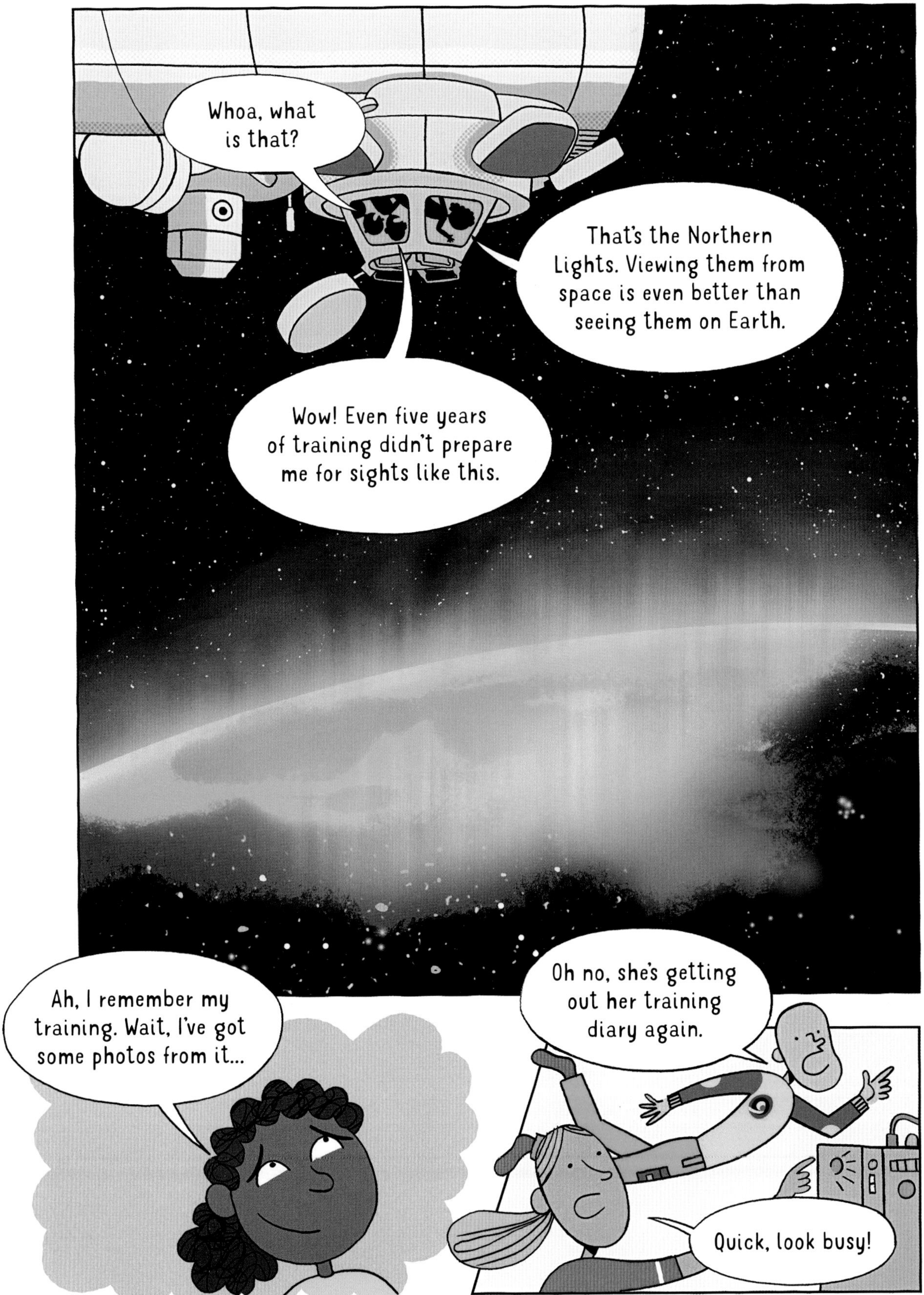
Whoa, what is that?
That's the Northern Lights. Viewing them from space is even better than seeing them on Earth.
Wow! Even five years of training didn't prepare me for sights like this.
Ah, I remember my training. Wait, I've got some photos from it...
Oh no, she's getting out her training diary again.
Quick, look busy!

BECKY'S TRAINING DIARY

Arriving at the space agency to begin five years of astronaut training!

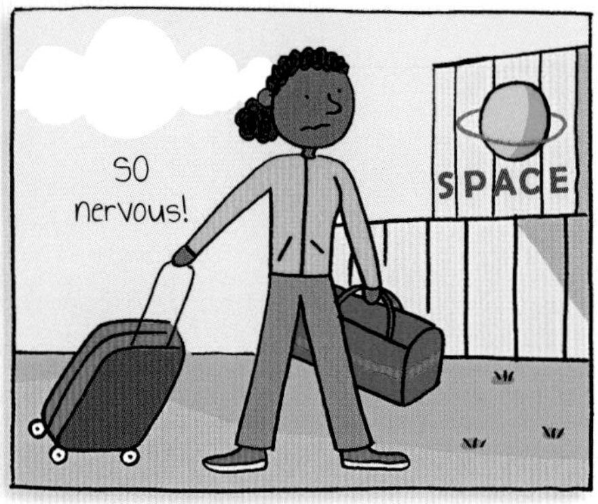
SO nervous!
SPACE

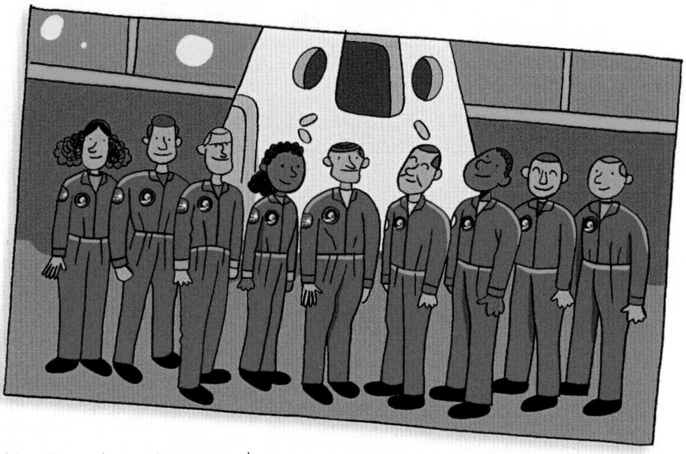

Meeting the other people hoping to become astronauts. Some were pilots or doctors, and some were engineers, like me.

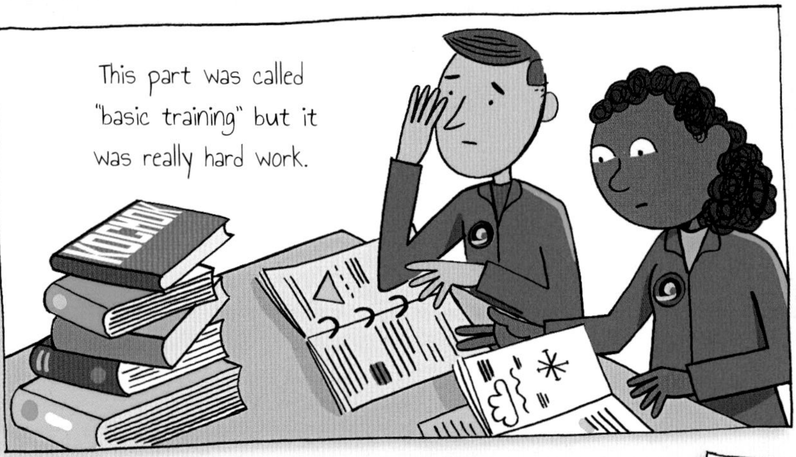
This part was called "basic training" but it was really hard work.

We spent HOURS learning how rockets and spacecraft work. We learned Russian, too, because some missions take off from Russia.

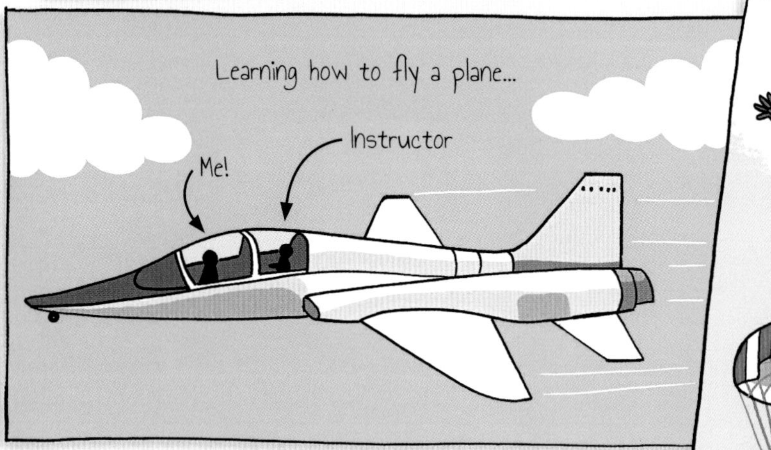
Learning how to fly a plane...
Instructor
Me!

This taught us to work in a cramped cockpit, like in some spacecraft.

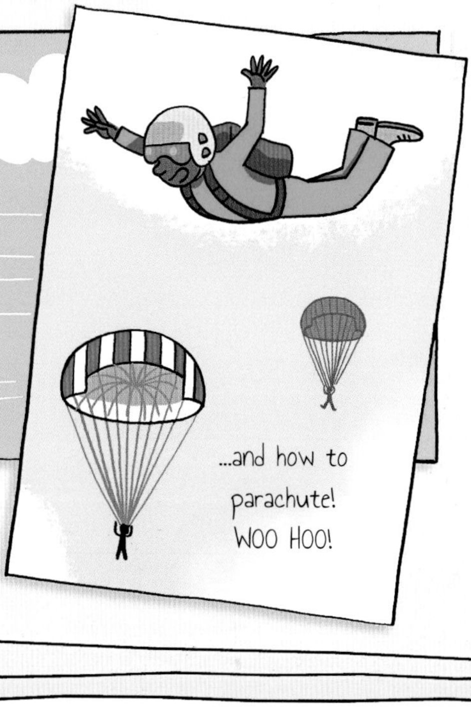
...and how to parachute! WOO HOO!

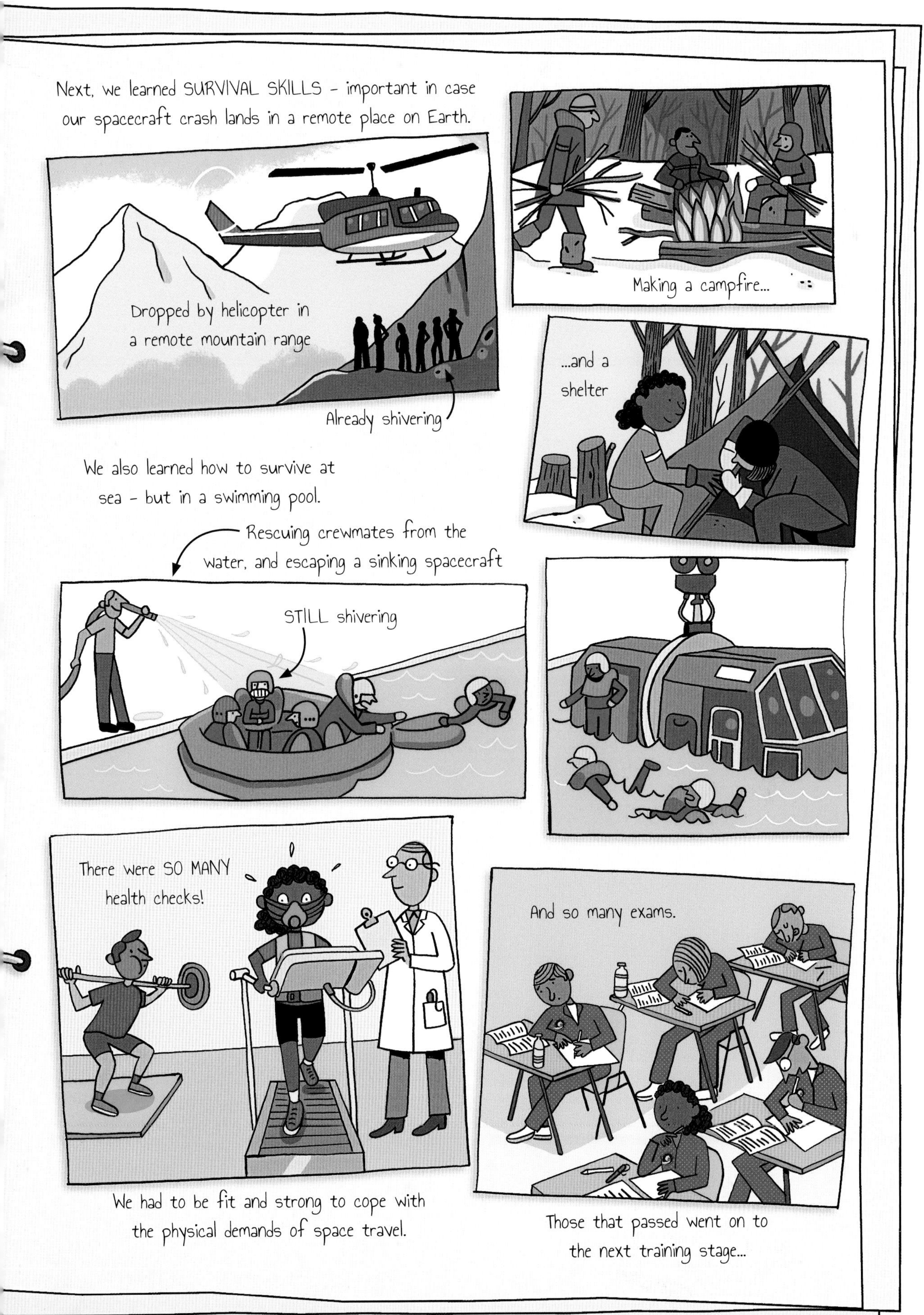
Next, we learned SURVIVAL SKILLS – important in case our spacecraft crash lands in a remote place on Earth.
Dropped by helicopter in a remote mountain range
Already shivering
Making a campfire...
...and a shelter
We also learned how to survive at sea – but in a swimming pool.
Rescuing crewmates from the water, and escaping a sinking spacecraft
STILL shivering
There were SO MANY health checks!
We had to be fit and strong to cope with the physical demands of space travel.
And so many exams.
Those that passed went on to the next training stage...

The next part of our training was in a full-size model of a SPACE STATION!

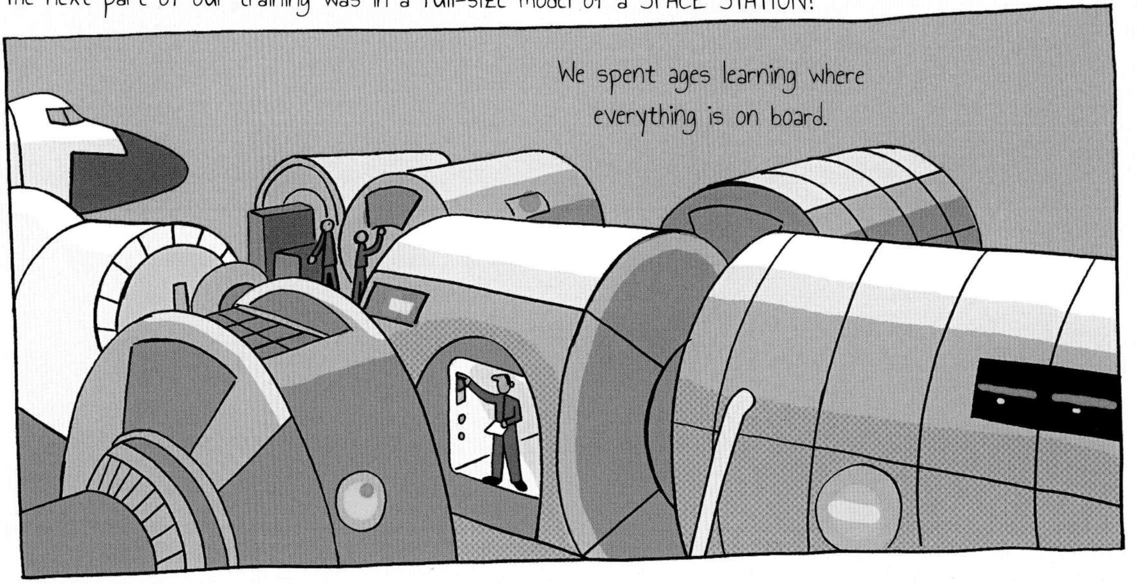
We spent ages learning where everything is on board.

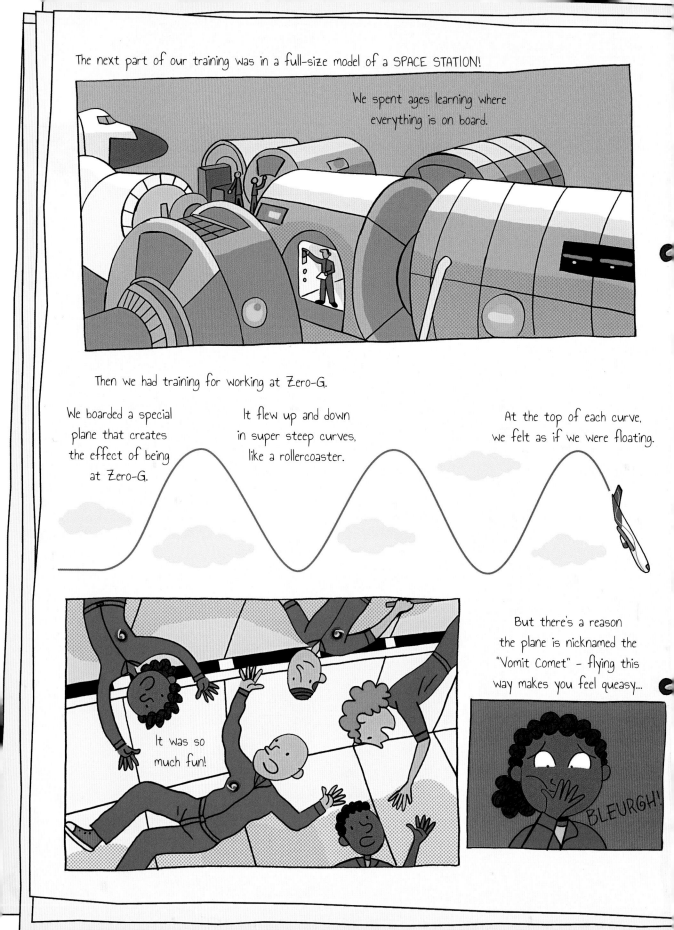

Then we had training for working at Zero-G.

We boarded a special plane that creates the effect of being at Zero-G.

It flew up and down in super steep curves, like a rollercoaster.

At the top of each curve, we felt as if we were floating.

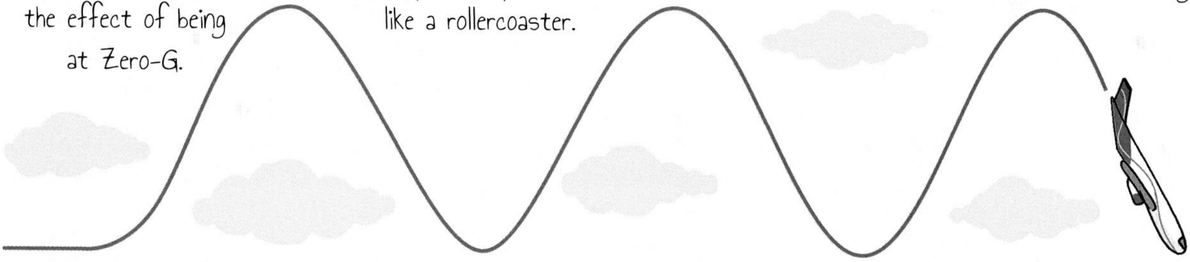

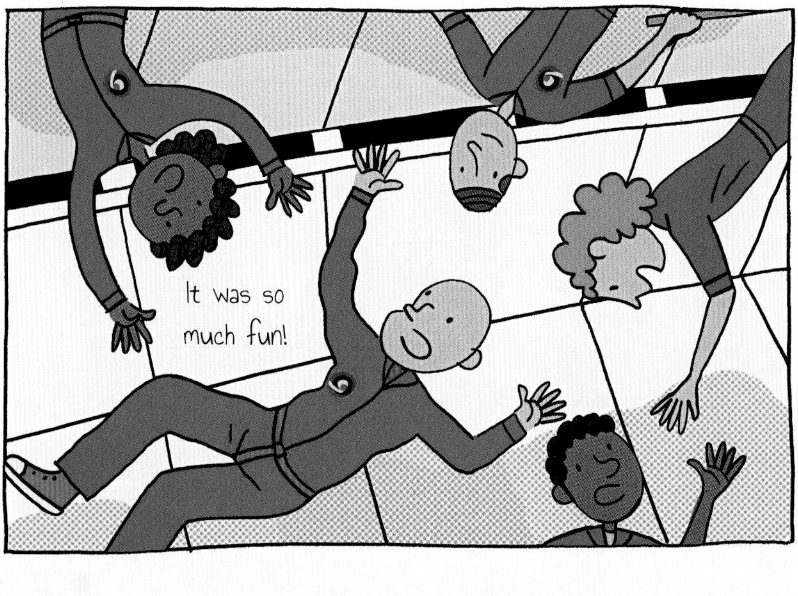
It was so much fun!

But there's a reason the plane is nicknamed the "Vomit Comet" – flying this way makes you feel queasy...

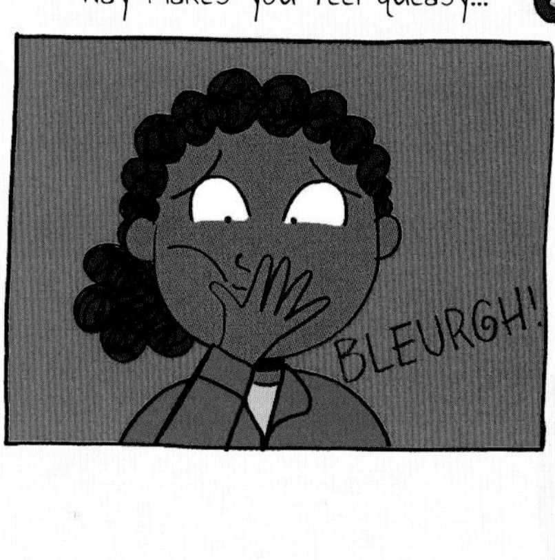
BLEURGH!

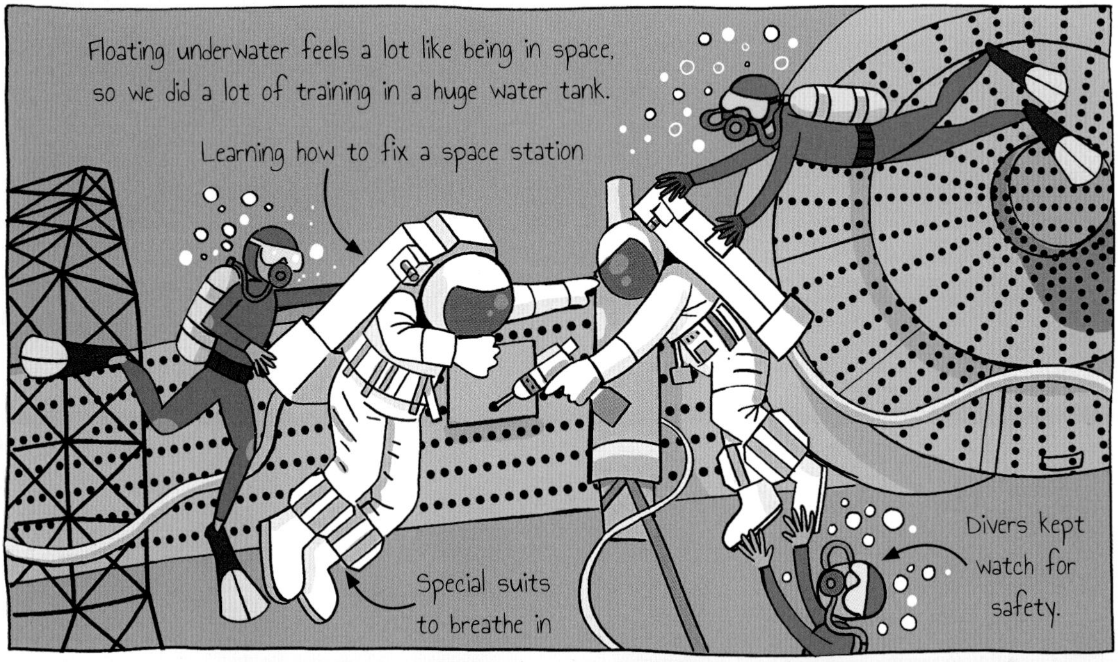
Floating underwater feels a lot like being in space, so we did a lot of training in a huge water tank.
Learning how to fix a space station
Special suits to breathe in
Divers kept watch for safety.

We also used high-tech virtual reality headsets.

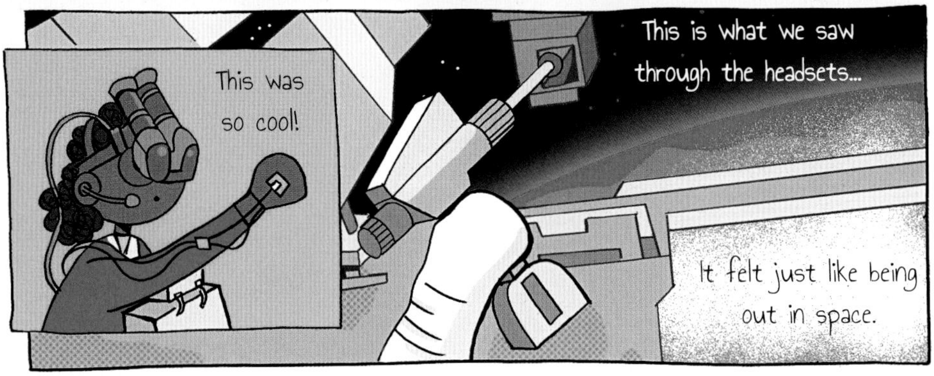
This was so cool!
This is what we saw through the headsets...
It felt just like being out in space.

Finally, we had to practice EVERY SINGLE THING we'd do on the space station.

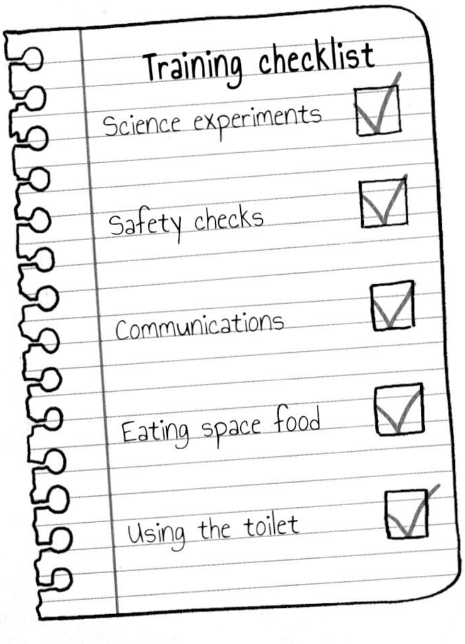
Training checklist
Science experiments
Safety checks
Communications
Eating space food
Using the toilet

This is the day I was selected for a mission to the REAL space station! Jane and Sergey were chosen, too!

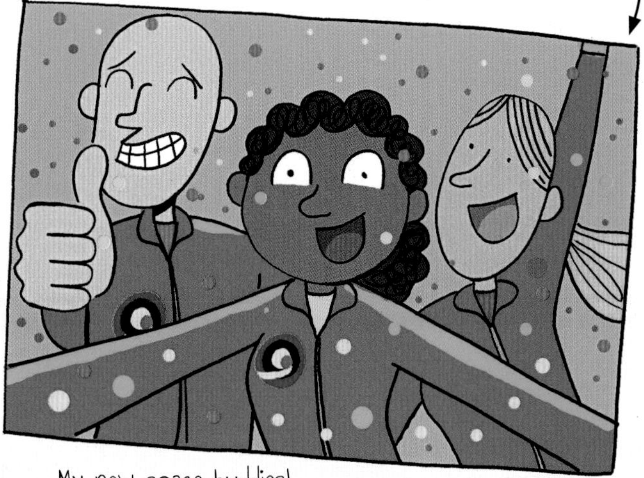

My new space buddies!

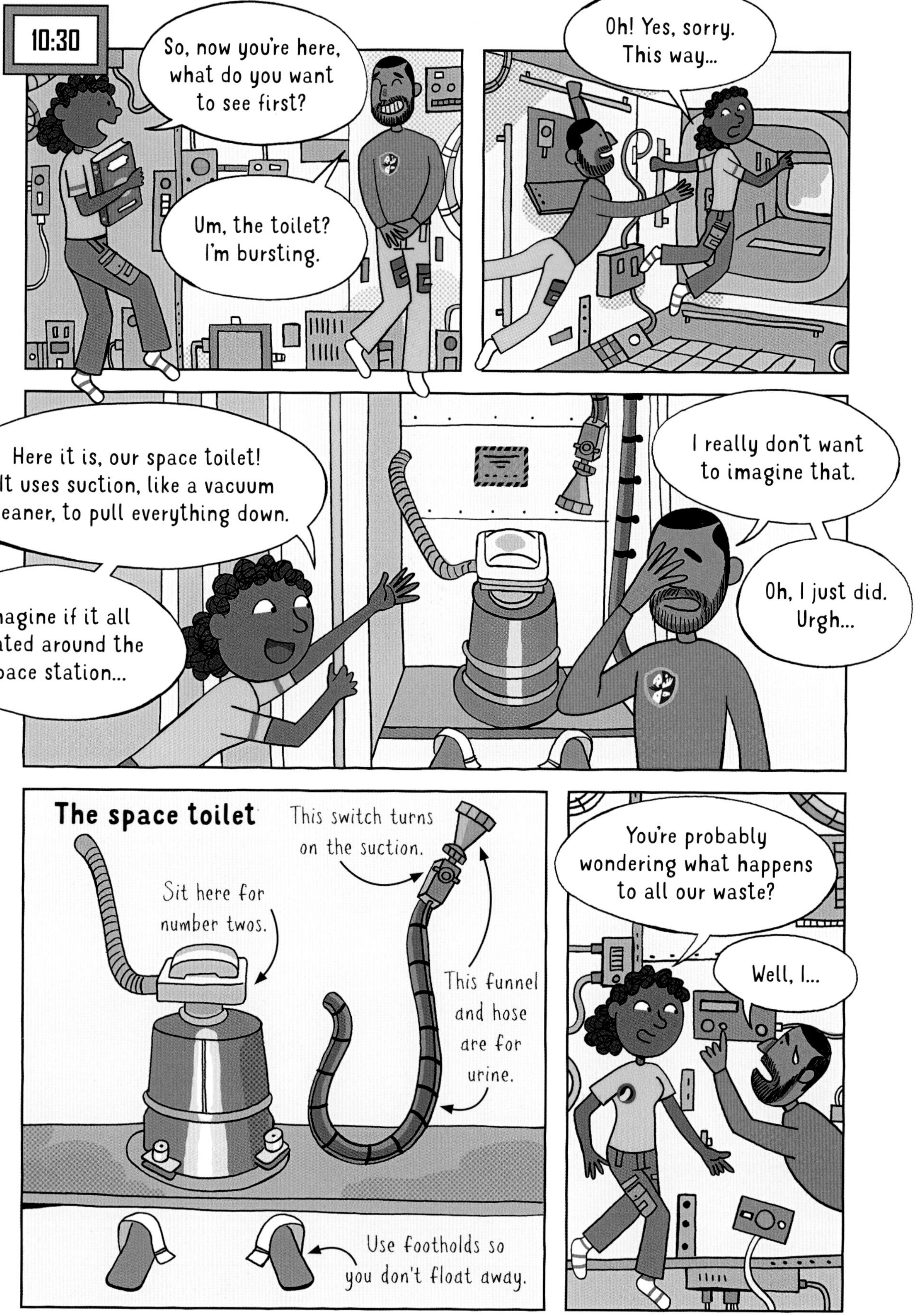
10:30
So, now you're here, what do you want to see first?
Um, the toilet? I'm bursting.
Oh! Yes, sorry. This way...
Here it is, our space toilet! It uses suction, like a vacuum cleaner, to pull everything down.
Imagine if it all floated around the space station...
I really don't want to imagine that.
Oh, I just did. Urgh...
The space toilet
Sit here for number twos.
This switch turns on the suction.
This funnel and hose are for urine.
Use footholds so you don't float away.
You're probably wondering what happens to all our waste?
Well, I...

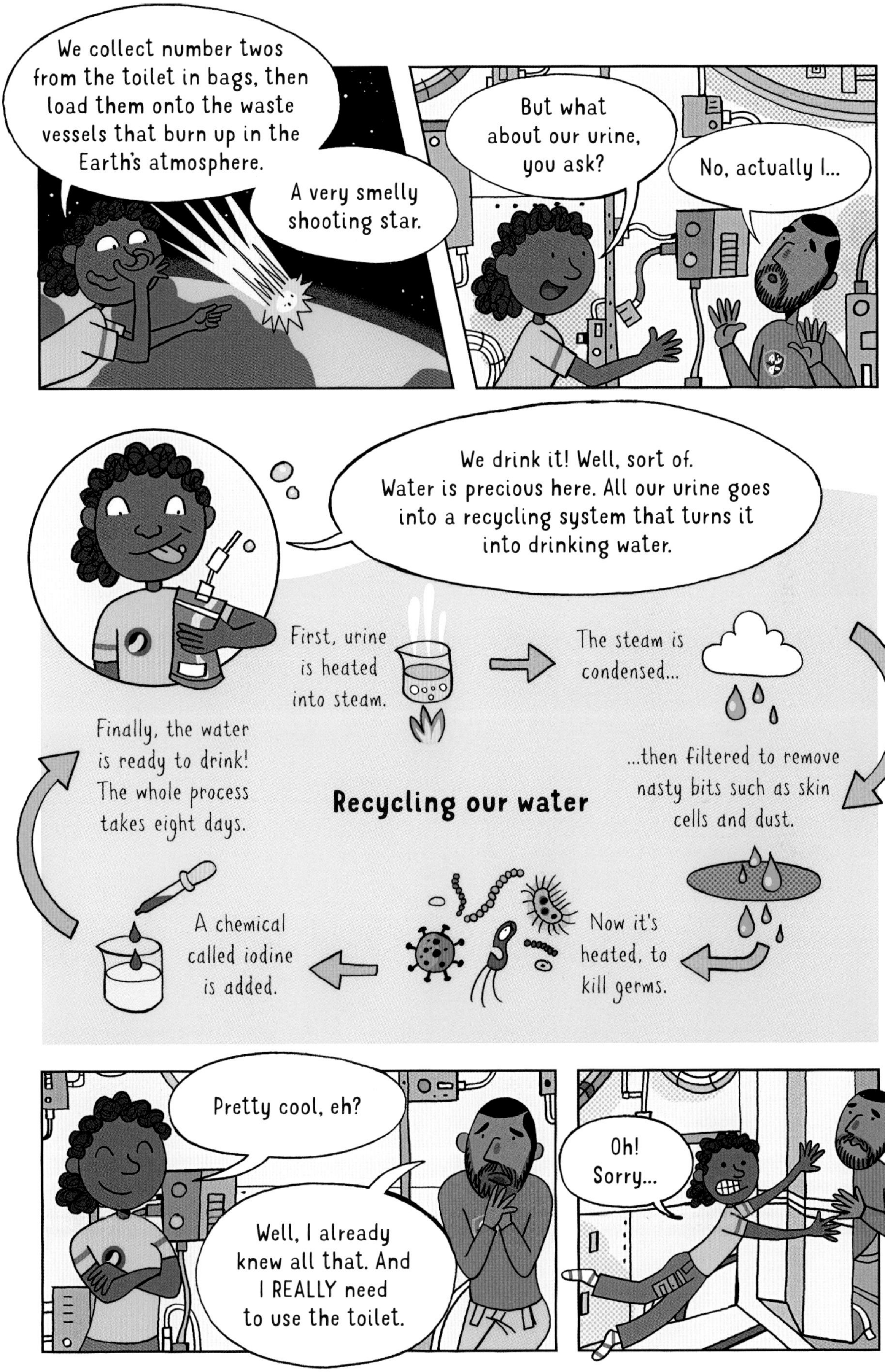
We collect number twos from the toilet in bags, then load them onto the waste vessels that burn up in the Earth's atmosphere.
A very smelly shooting star.
But what about our urine, you ask?
No, actually I...
We drink it! Well, sort of. Water is precious here. All our urine goes into a recycling system that turns it into drinking water.
Recycling our water
First, urine is heated into steam.
The steam is condensed...
...then filtered to remove nasty bits such as skin cells and dust.
Now it's heated, to kill germs.
A chemical called iodine is added.
Finally, the water is ready to drink! The whole process takes eight days.
Pretty cool, eh?
Well, I already knew all that. And I REALLY need to use the toilet.
Oh! Sorry...

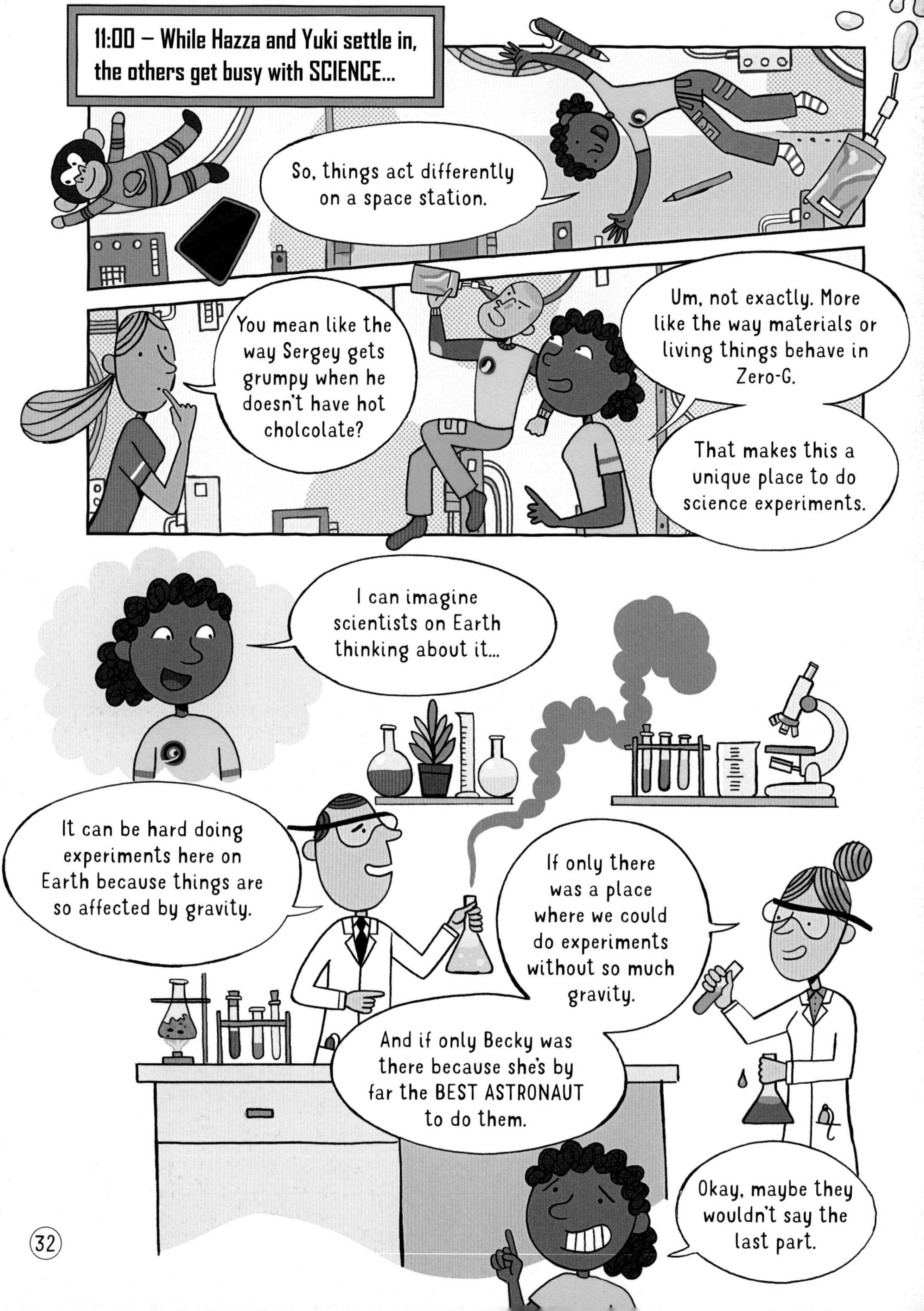
11:00 – While Hazza and Yuki settle in, the others get busy with SCIENCE...
So, things act differently on a space station.
You mean like the way Sergey gets grumpy when he doesn't have hot cholcolate?
Um, not exactly. More like the way materials or living things behave in Zero-G.
That makes this a unique place to do science experiments.
I can imagine scientists on Earth thinking about it...
It can be hard doing experiments here on Earth because things are so affected by gravity.
If only there was a place where we could do experiments without so much gravity.
And if only Becky was there because she's by far the BEST ASTRONAUT to do them.
Okay, maybe they wouldn't say the last part.

Uses of space science

Experiments done in space have helped improve people's lives on Earth in all sorts of ways. Here are just a few:

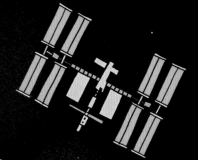

Advancing laser eye surgery...

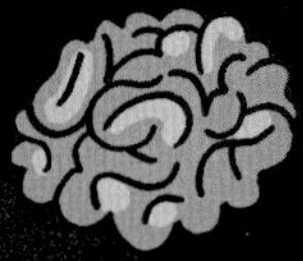

...and brain surgery, too

Developing new metals to build lighter aircraft...

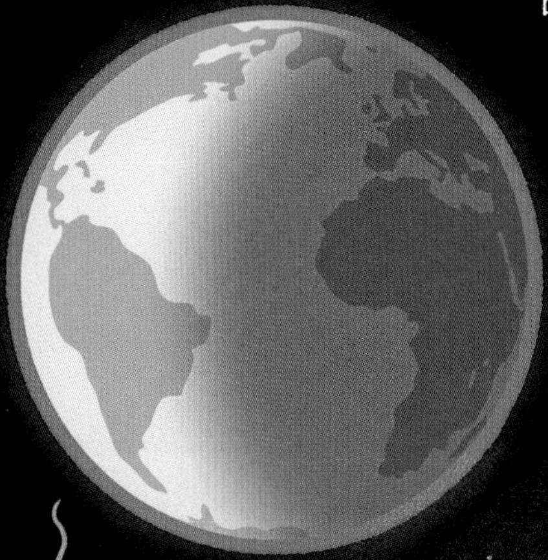

Helping design better scanners for hospitals

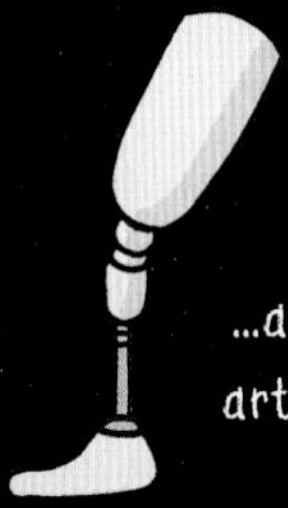

...and stronger artificial limbs

Stopping sweaty clothes from being so smelly

Creating more efficient water recycling systems

Other experiments test ways to make space travel safer, so we can explore deeper...

...and deeper

...into the solar system.

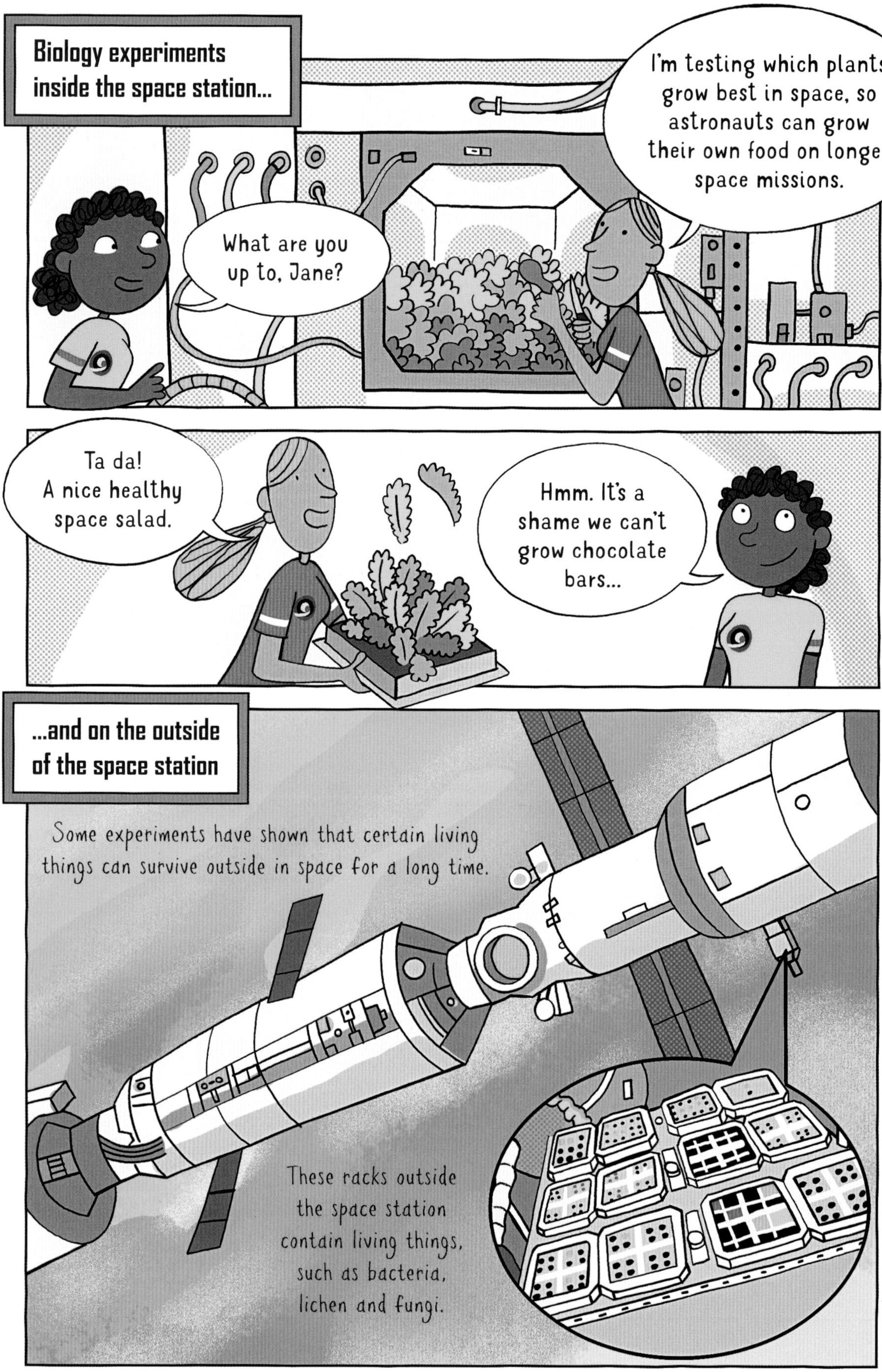
Biology experiments inside the space station...
What are you up to, Jane?
I'm testing which plants grow best in space, so astronauts can grow their own food on longer space missions.
Ta da! A nice healthy space salad.
Hmm. It's a shame we can't grow chocolate bars...
...and on the outside of the space station
Some experiments have shown that certain living things can survive outside in space for a long time.
These racks outside the space station contain living things, such as bacteria, lichen and fungi.

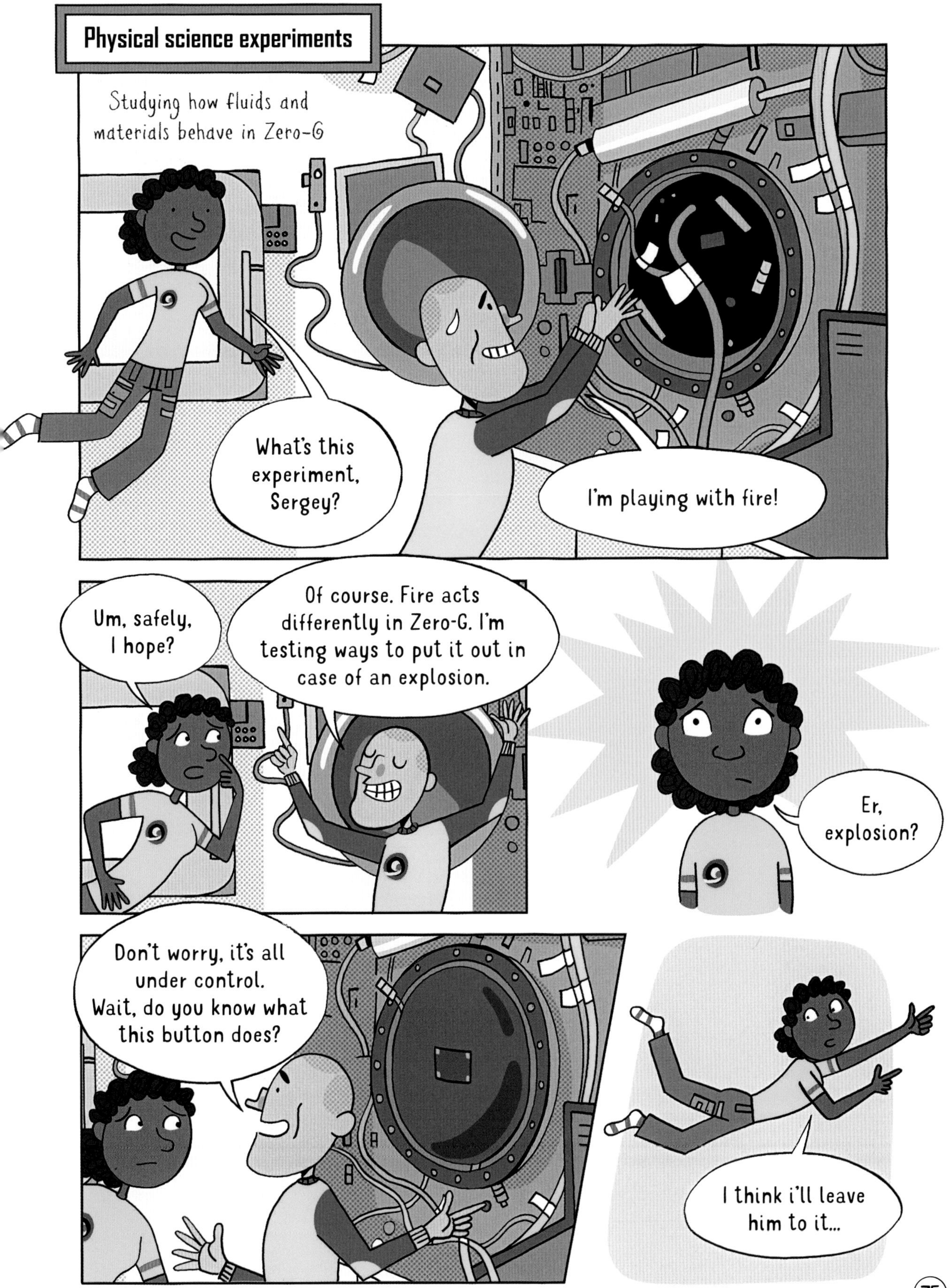
Physical science experiments
Studying how fluids and materials behave in Zero-G
What's this experiment, Sergey?
I'm playing with fire!
Um, safely, I hope?
Of course. Fire acts differently in Zero-G. I'm testing ways to put it out in case of an explosion.
Er, explosion?
Don't worry, it's all under control. Wait, do you know what this button does?
I think i'll leave him to it...

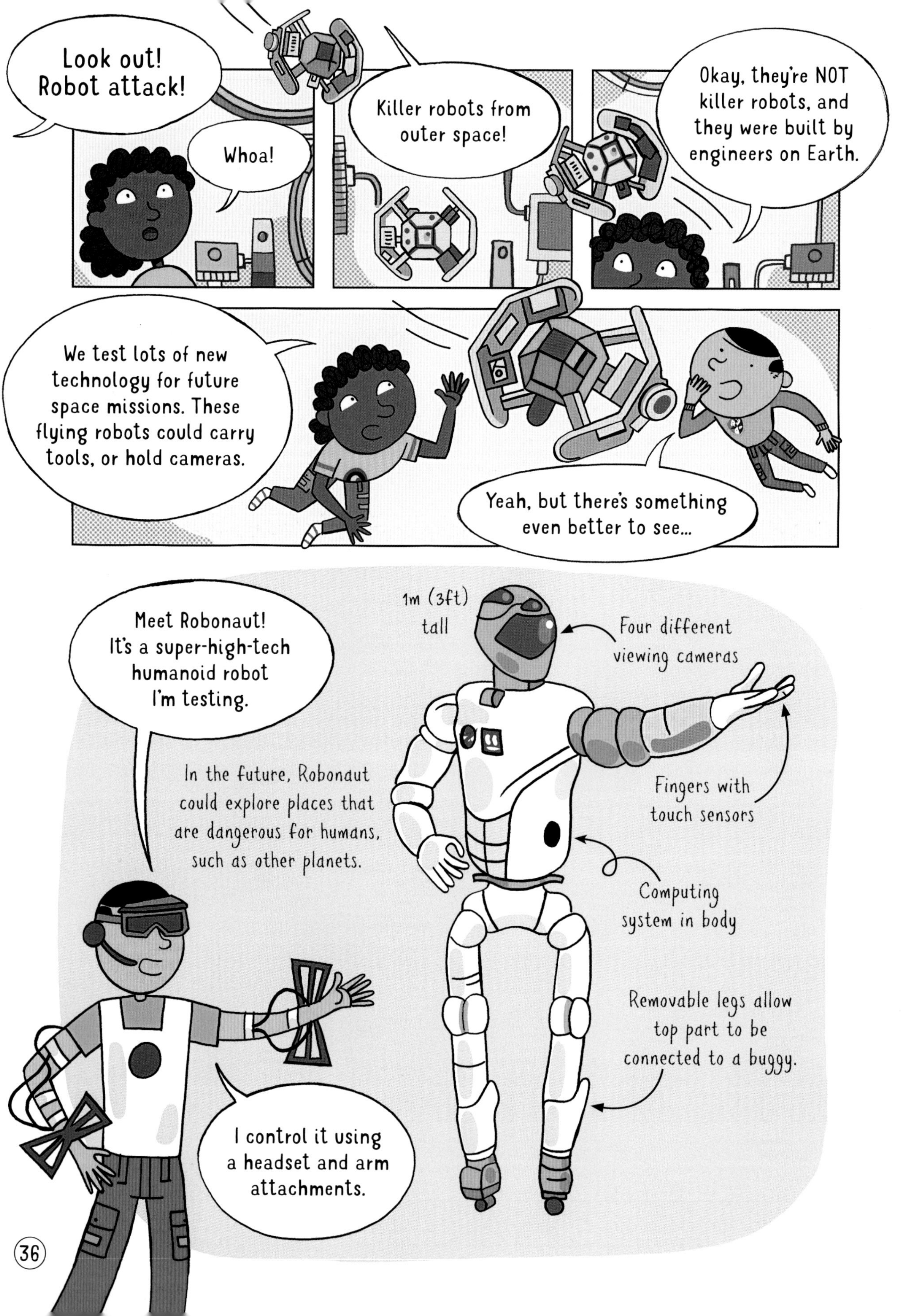

Look out! Robot attack!
Whoa!
Killer robots from outer space!
Okay, they're NOT killer robots, and they were built by engineers on Earth.
We test lots of new technology for future space missions. These flying robots could carry tools, or hold cameras.
Yeah, but there's something even better to see...
Meet Robonaut! It's a super-high-tech humanoid robot I'm testing.
1m (3ft) tall
Four different viewing cameras
In the future, Robonaut could explore places that are dangerous for humans, such as other planets.
Fingers with touch sensors
Computing system in body
Removable legs allow top part to be connected to a buggy.
I control it using a headset and arm attachments.

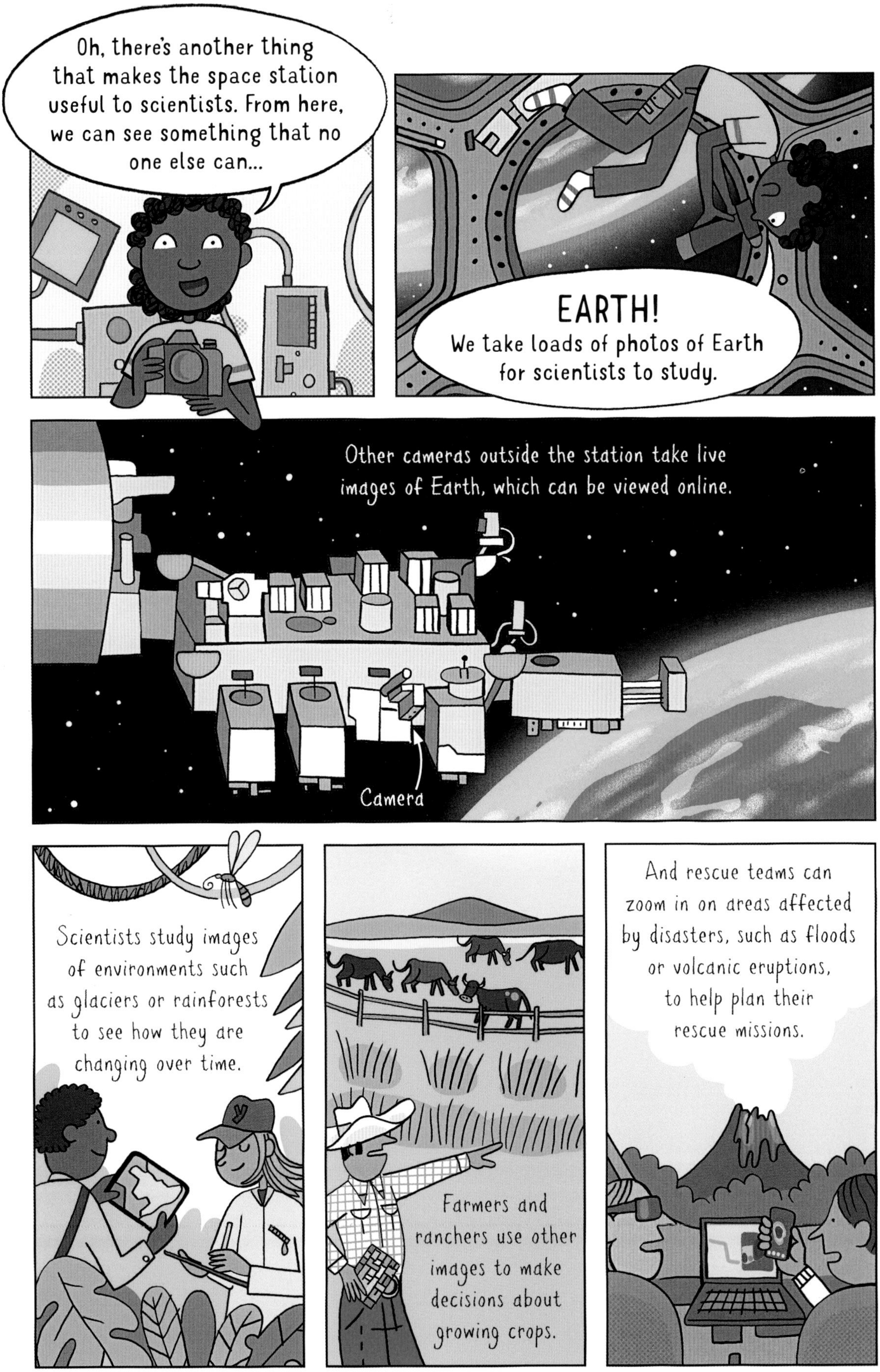
Oh, there's another thing that makes the space station useful to scientists. From here, we can see something that no one else can...
EARTH!
We take loads of photos of Earth for scientists to study.
Other cameras outside the station take live images of Earth, which can be viewed online.
Camera
Scientists study images of environments such as glaciers or rainforests to see how they are changing over time.
Farmers and ranchers use other images to make decisions about growing crops.
And rescue teams can zoom in on areas affected by disasters, such as floods or volcanic eruptions, to help plan their rescue missions.

More space station science

A new type of fire

This experiment looked at how different fuels burned at Zero-G.

One fuel continued burning even after it appeared to go out. The astronauts had made INVISIBLE FIRE!

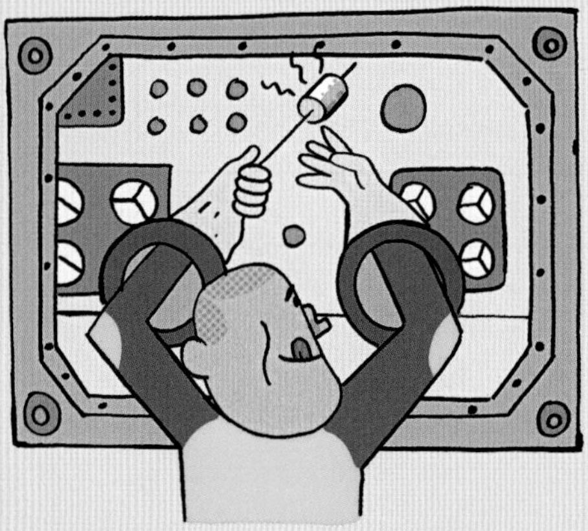

Here, Sergey is toasting a marshmallow over invisible fire.

(Okay, this part of the experiment didn't actually happen, but it would have been cool!)

The discovery could help scientists on Earth make engines that are less damaging to the environment.

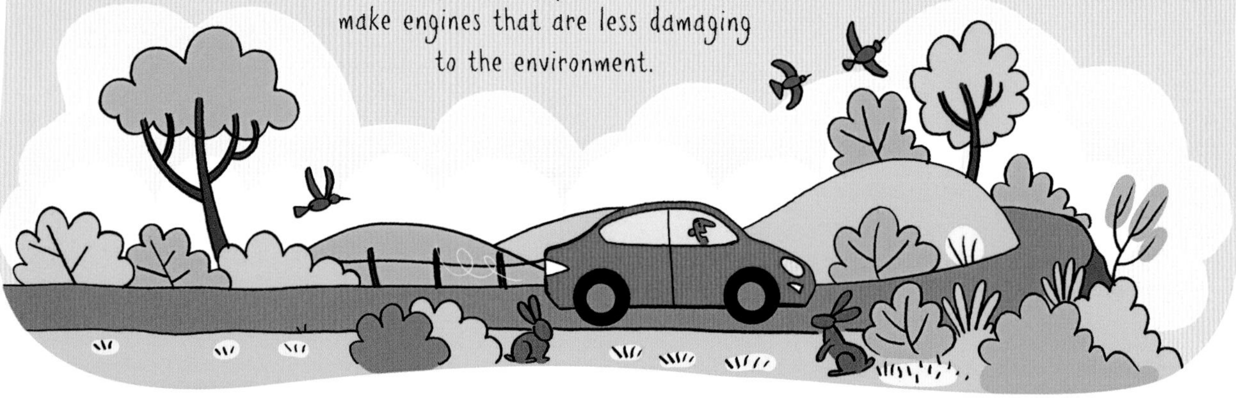

How it all began

Another experiment super-cooled atoms and studied how they behaved in Zero-G.

This showed how the Universe may have begun.

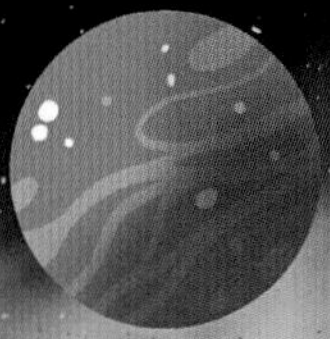

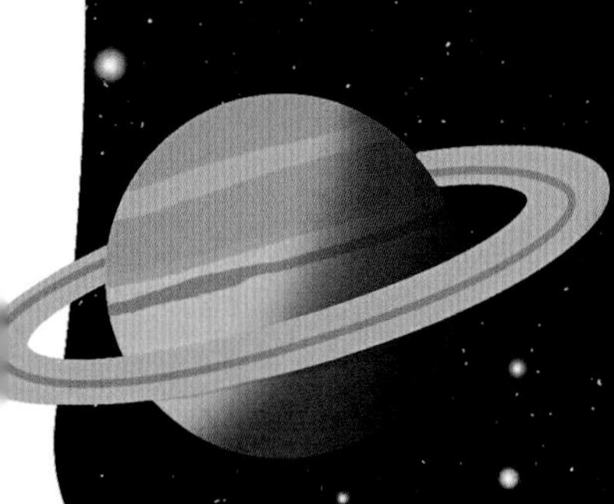

Astronauts also zapped space dust with electricity, and observed how it stuck together.

This gave us a glimpse of how planets start to form.

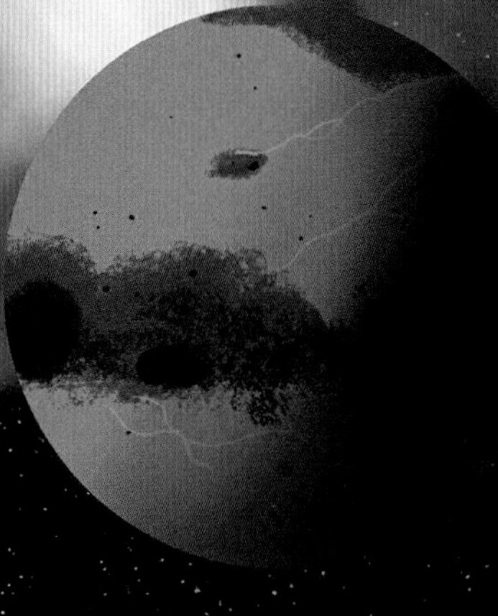

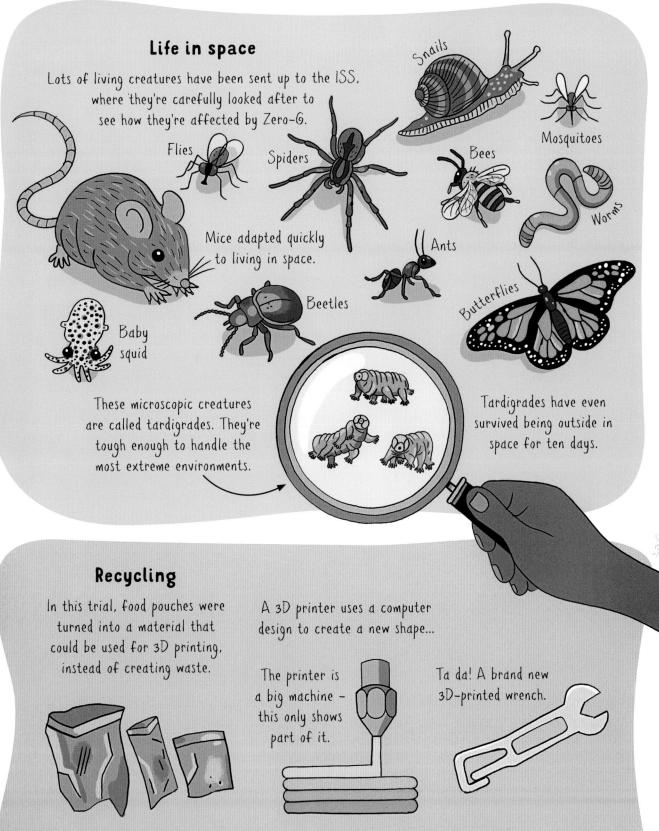

Life in space

Lots of living creatures have been sent up to the ISS, where they're carefully looked after to see how they're affected by Zero-G.

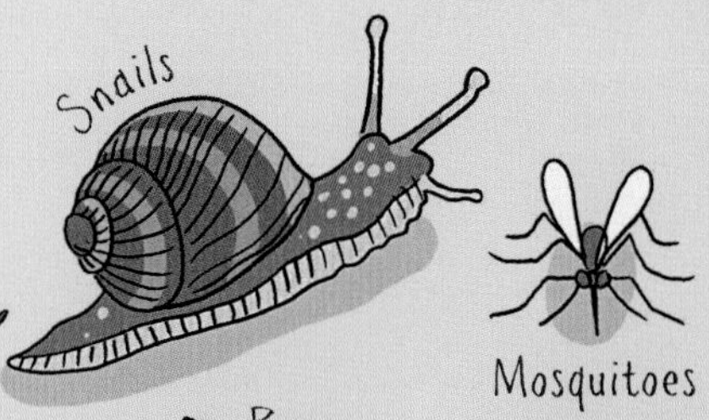
Snails
Mosquitoes

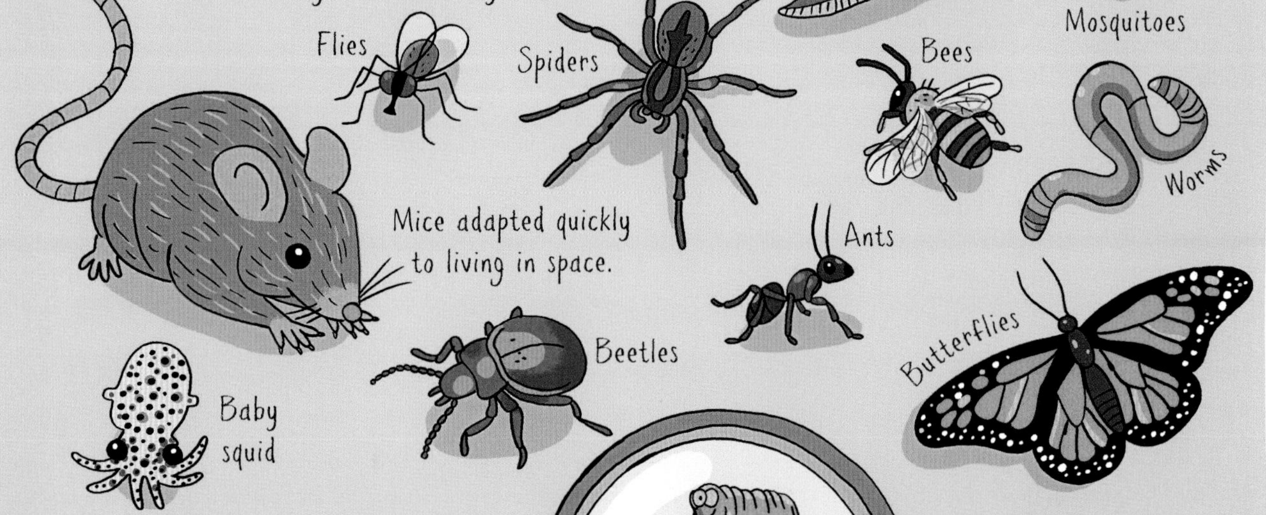
Flies
Spiders
Bees
Worms
Mice adapted quickly to living in space.
Ants
Butterflies
Beetles
Baby squid

These microscopic creatures are called tardigrades. They're tough enough to handle the most extreme environments.

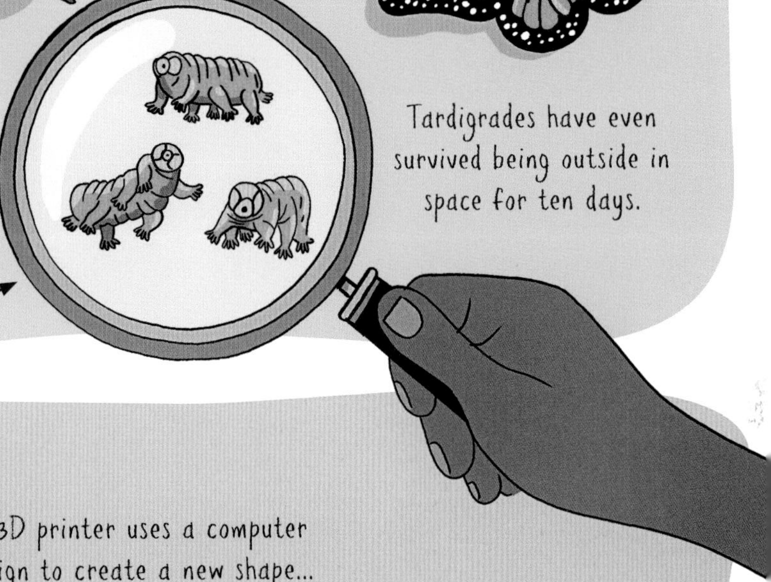

Tardigrades have even survived being outside in space for ten days.

Recycling

In this trial, food pouches were turned into a material that could be used for 3D printing, instead of creating waste.

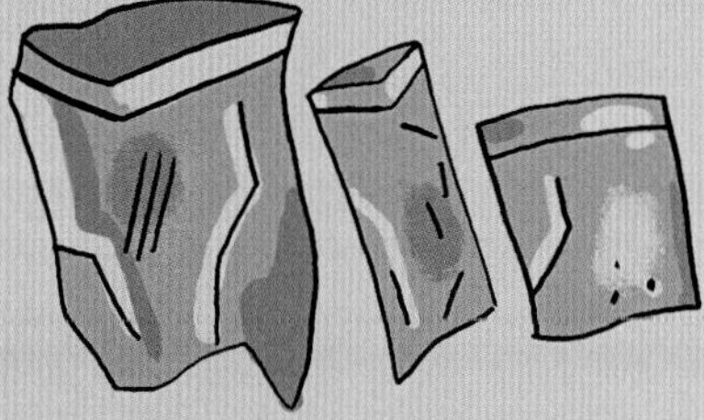

A 3D printer uses a computer design to create a new shape...

The printer is a big machine – this only shows part of it.

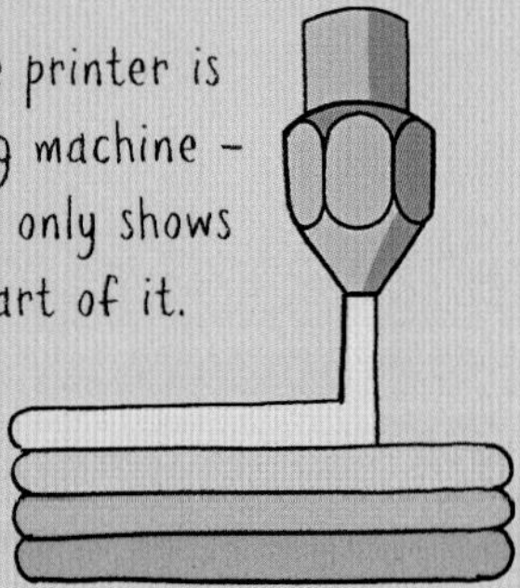

Ta da! A brand new 3D-printed wrench.

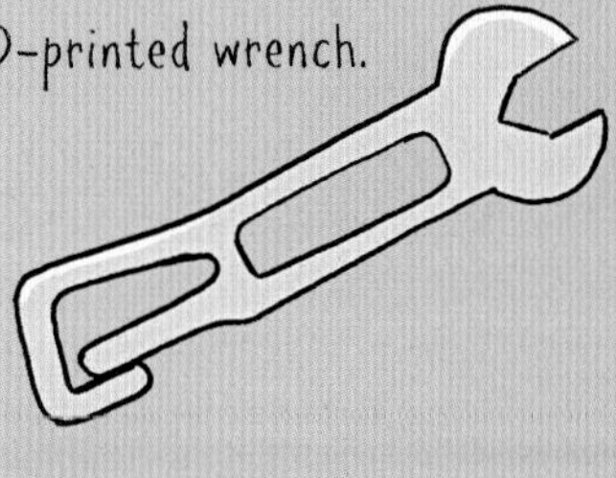

This could be really useful to astronauts on long journeys into space. They won't be able to get supplies from Earth, so they'll need to make their own.

13:00 - Staying strong in space

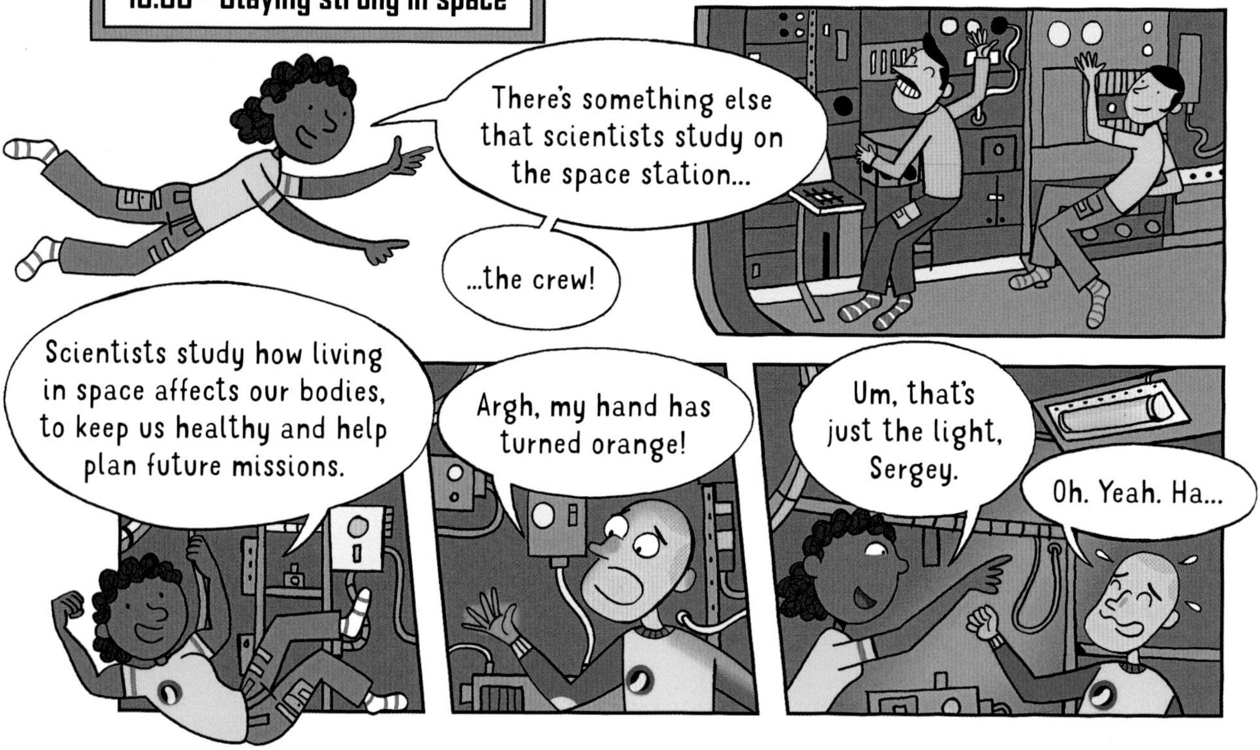

There's something else that scientists study on the space station...
...the crew!
Scientists study how living in space affects our bodies, to keep us healthy and help plan future missions.
Argh, my hand has turned orange!
Um, that's just the light, Sergey.
Oh. Yeah. Ha...

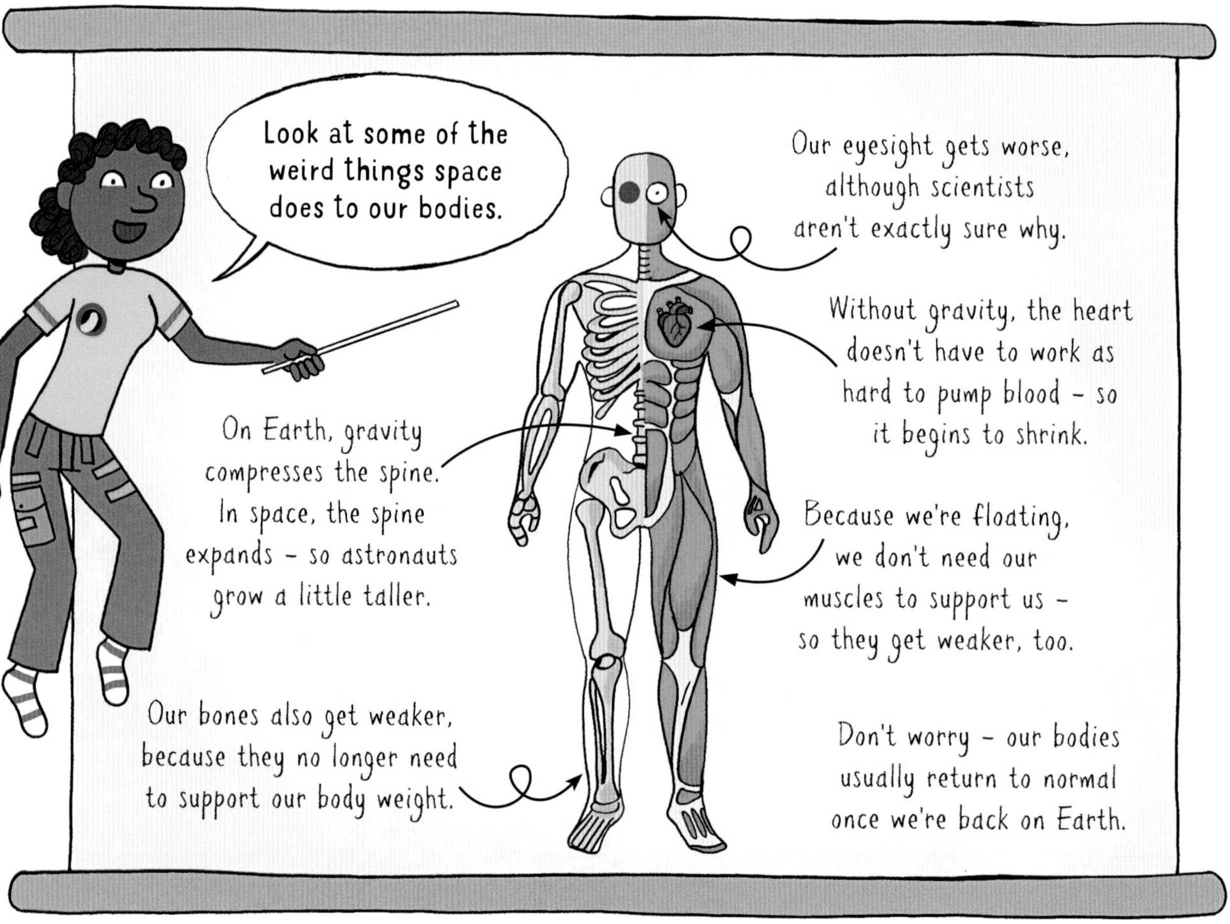

Look at some of the weird things space does to our bodies.
Our eyesight gets worse, although scientists aren't exactly sure why.
Without gravity, the heart doesn't have to work as hard to pump blood – so it begins to shrink.
On Earth, gravity compresses the spine. In space, the spine expands – so astronauts grow a little taller.
Because we're floating, we don't need our muscles to support us – so they get weaker, too.
Our bones also get weaker, because they no longer need to support our body weight.
Don't worry – our bodies usually return to normal once we're back on Earth.

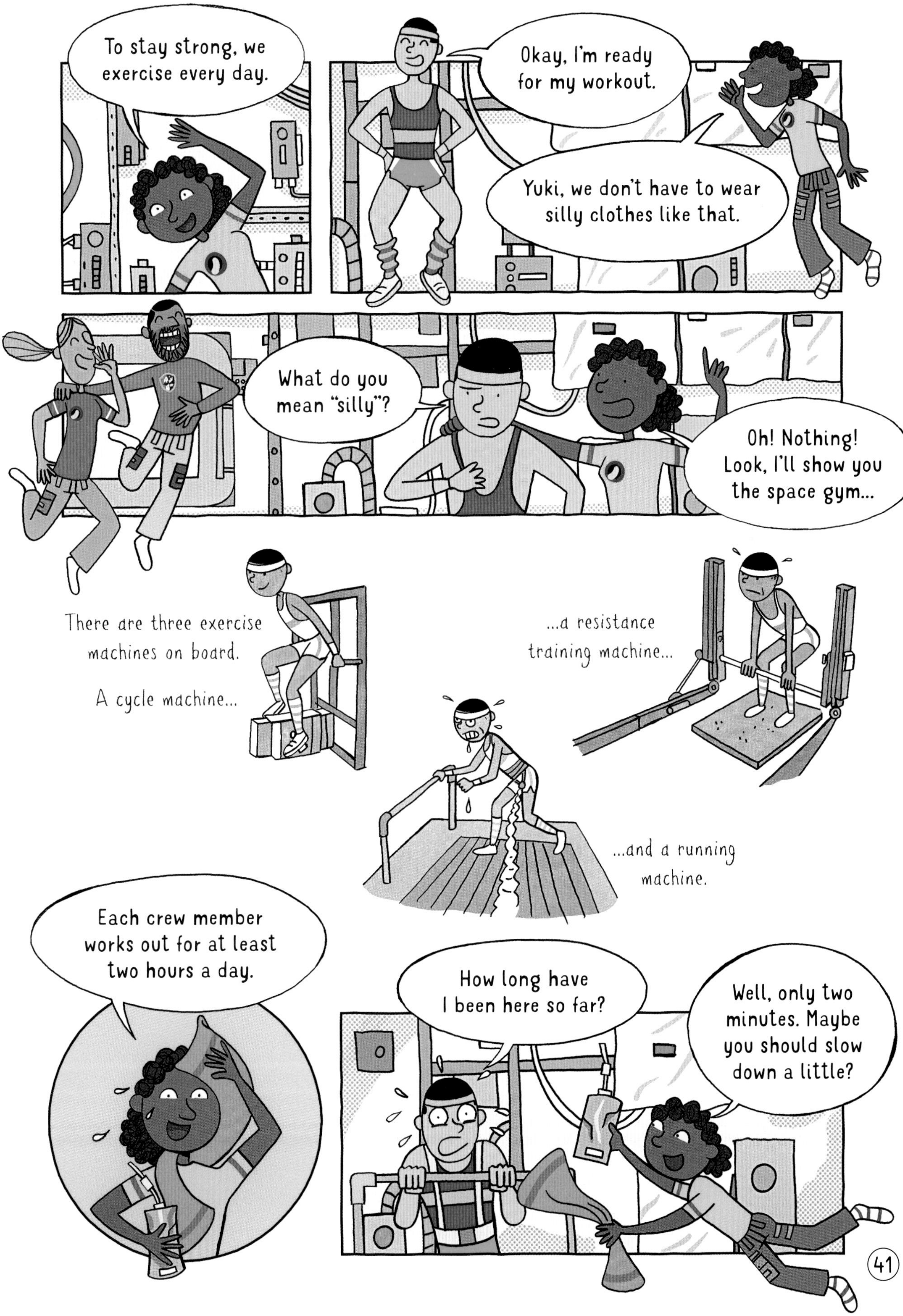

To stay strong, we exercise every day.
Okay, I'm ready for my workout.
Yuki, we don't have to wear silly clothes like that.
What do you mean "silly"?
Oh! Nothing! Look, I'll show you the space gym...
There are three exercise machines on board.
A cycle machine...
...a resistance training machine...
...and a running machine.
Each crew member works out for at least two hours a day.
How long have I been here so far?
Well, only two minutes. Maybe you should slow down a little?

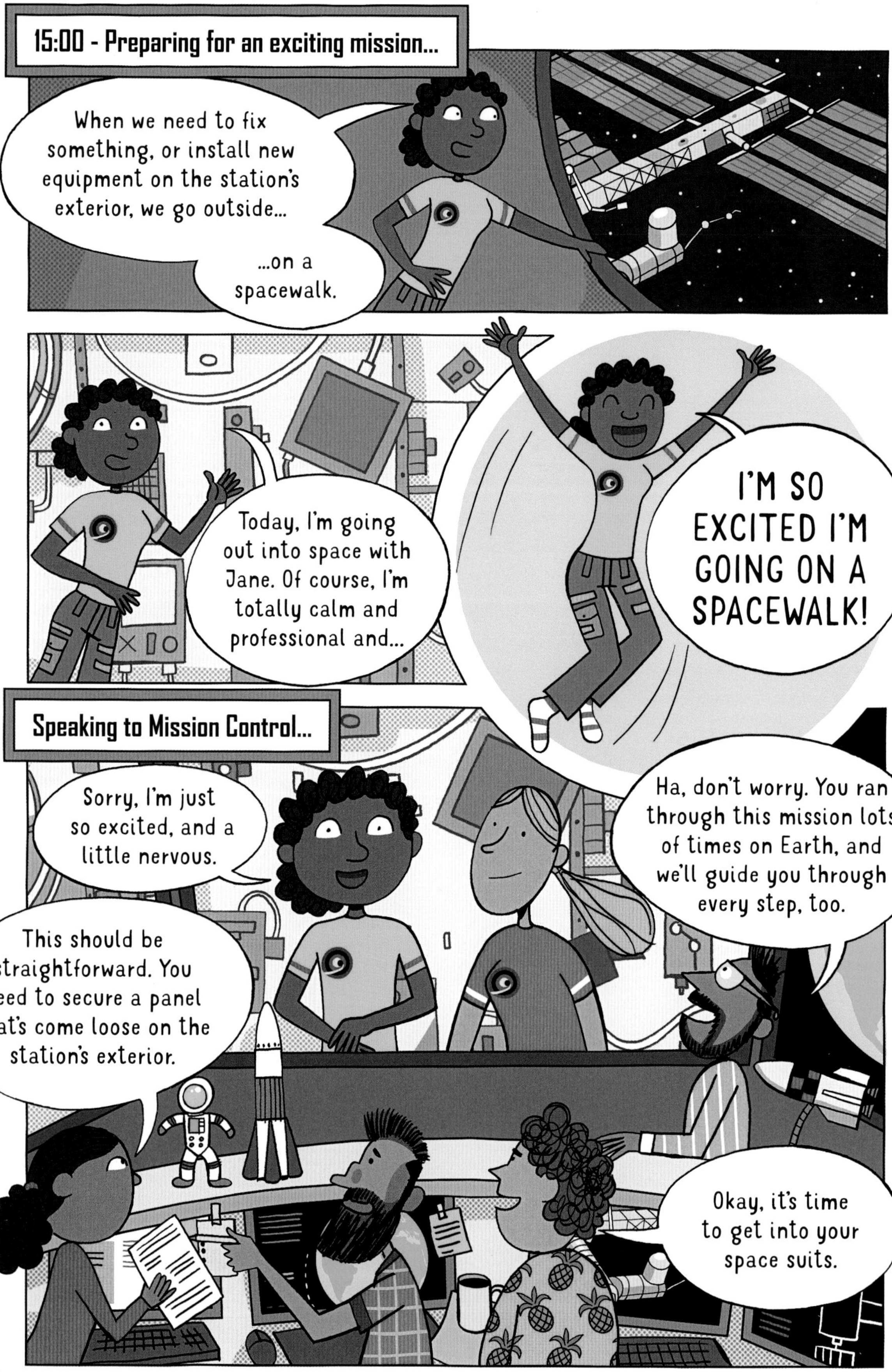
15:00 - Preparing for an exciting mission...
When we need to fix something, or install new equipment on the station's exterior, we go outside...
...on a spacewalk.
Today, I'm going out into space with Jane. Of course, I'm totally calm and professional and...
I'M SO EXCITED I'M GOING ON A SPACEWALK!
Speaking to Mission Control...
Sorry, I'm just so excited, and a little nervous.
Ha, don't worry. You ran through this mission lots of times on Earth, and we'll guide you through every step, too.
This should be straightforward. You need to secure a panel that's come loose on the station's exterior.
Okay, it's time to get into your space suits.

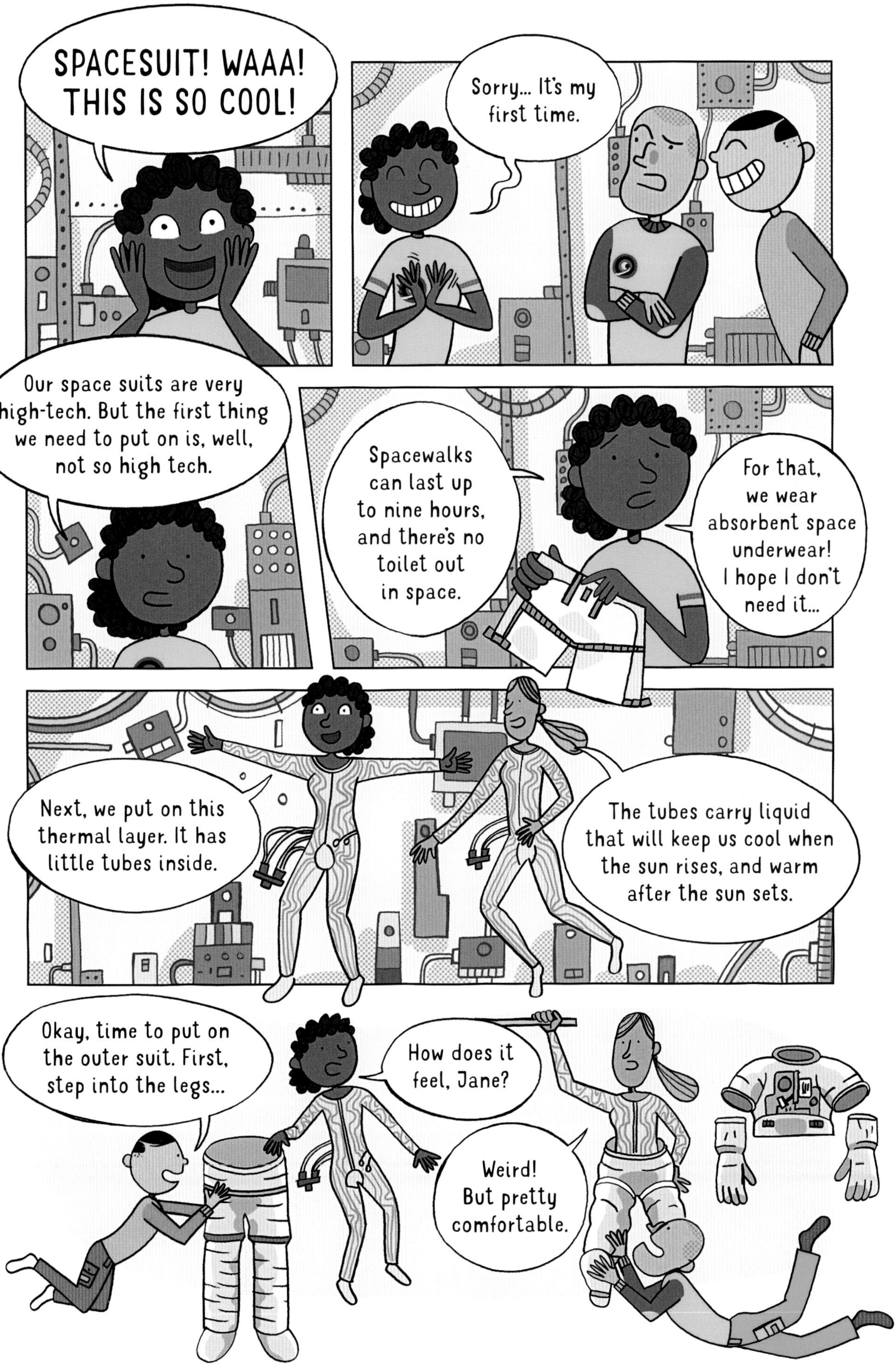

SPACESUIT! WAAA! THIS IS SO COOL!
Sorry... It's my first time.
Our space suits are very high-tech. But the first thing we need to put on is, well, not so high tech.
Spacewalks can last up to nine hours, and there's no toilet out in space.
For that, we wear absorbent space underwear! I hope I don't need it...
Next, we put on this thermal layer. It has little tubes inside.
The tubes carry liquid that will keep us cool when the sun rises, and warm after the sun sets.
Okay, time to put on the outer suit. First, step into the legs...
How does it feel, Jane?
Weird! But pretty comfortable.

Spacesuit

This type of suit is called an EMU (Extravehicular Mobility Unit). It's basically a mini spacecraft that keeps astronauts totally safe out in space.

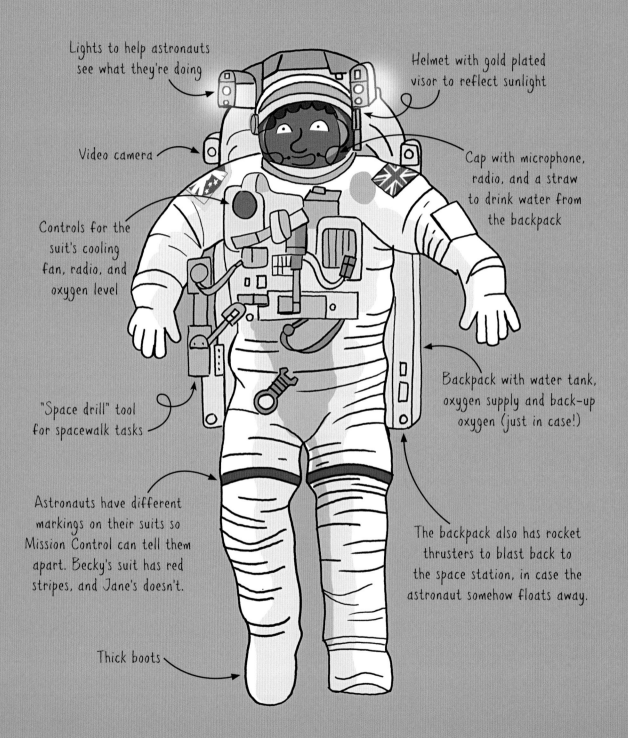

Lights to help astronauts see what they're doing

Helmet with gold plated visor to reflect sunlight

Video camera

Cap with microphone, radio, and a straw to drink water from the backpack

Controls for the suit's cooling fan, radio, and oxygen level

Backpack with water tank, oxygen supply and back-up oxygen (just in case!)

"Space drill" tool for spacewalk tasks

Astronauts have different markings on their suits so Mission Control can tell them apart. Becky's suit has red stripes, and Jane's doesn't.

The backpack also has rocket thrusters to blast back to the space station, in case the astronaut somehow floats away.

Thick boots

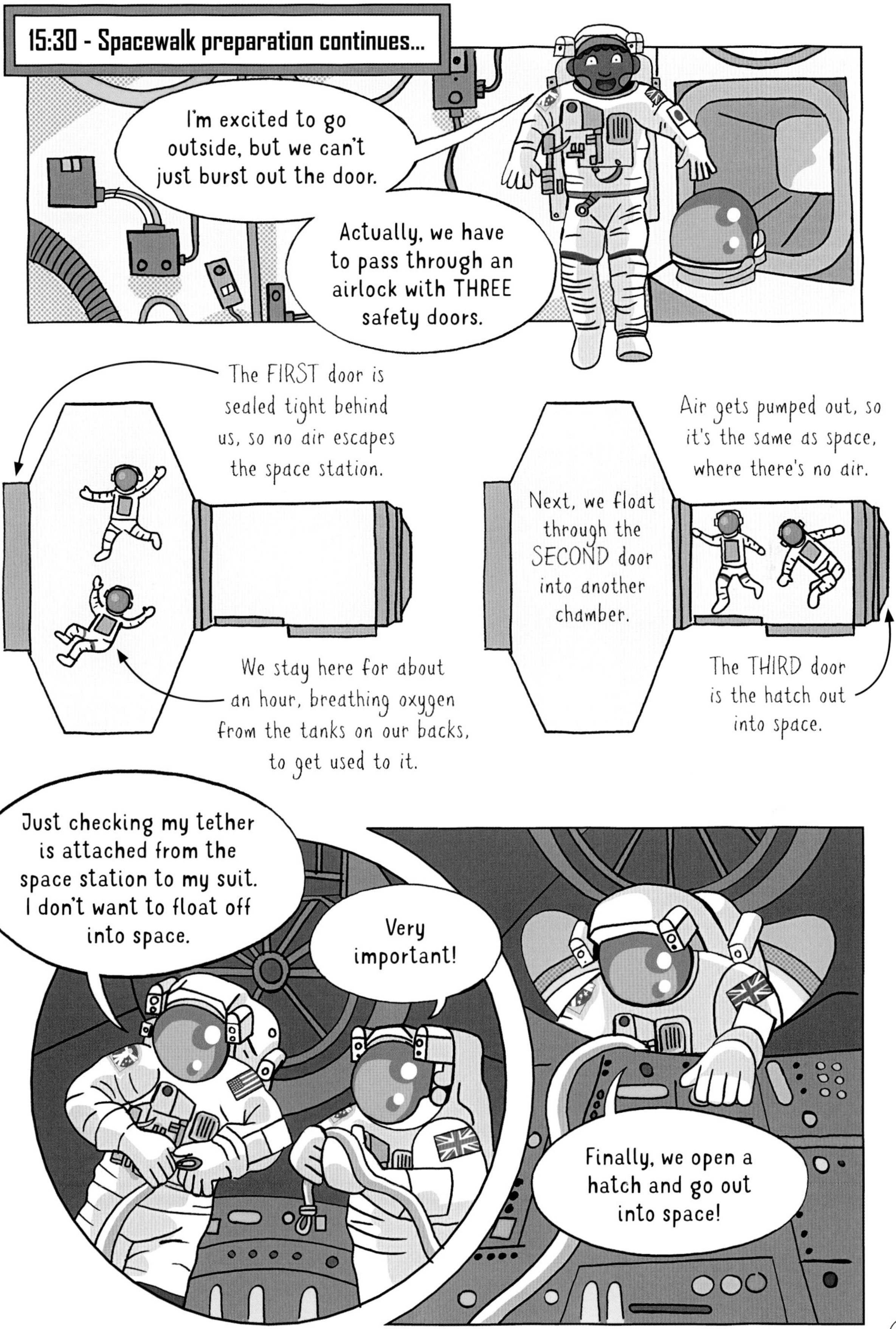
15:30 - Spacewalk preparation continues...
I'm excited to go outside, but we can't just burst out the door.
Actually, we have to pass through an airlock with THREE safety doors.
The FIRST door is sealed tight behind us, so no air escapes the space station.
We stay here for about an hour, breathing oxygen from the tanks on our backs, to get used to it.
Air gets pumped out, so it's the same as space, where there's no air.
Next, we float through the SECOND door into another chamber.
The THIRD door is the hatch out into space.
Just checking my tether is attached from the space station to my suit. I don't want to float off into space.
Very important!
Finally, we open a hatch and go out into space!

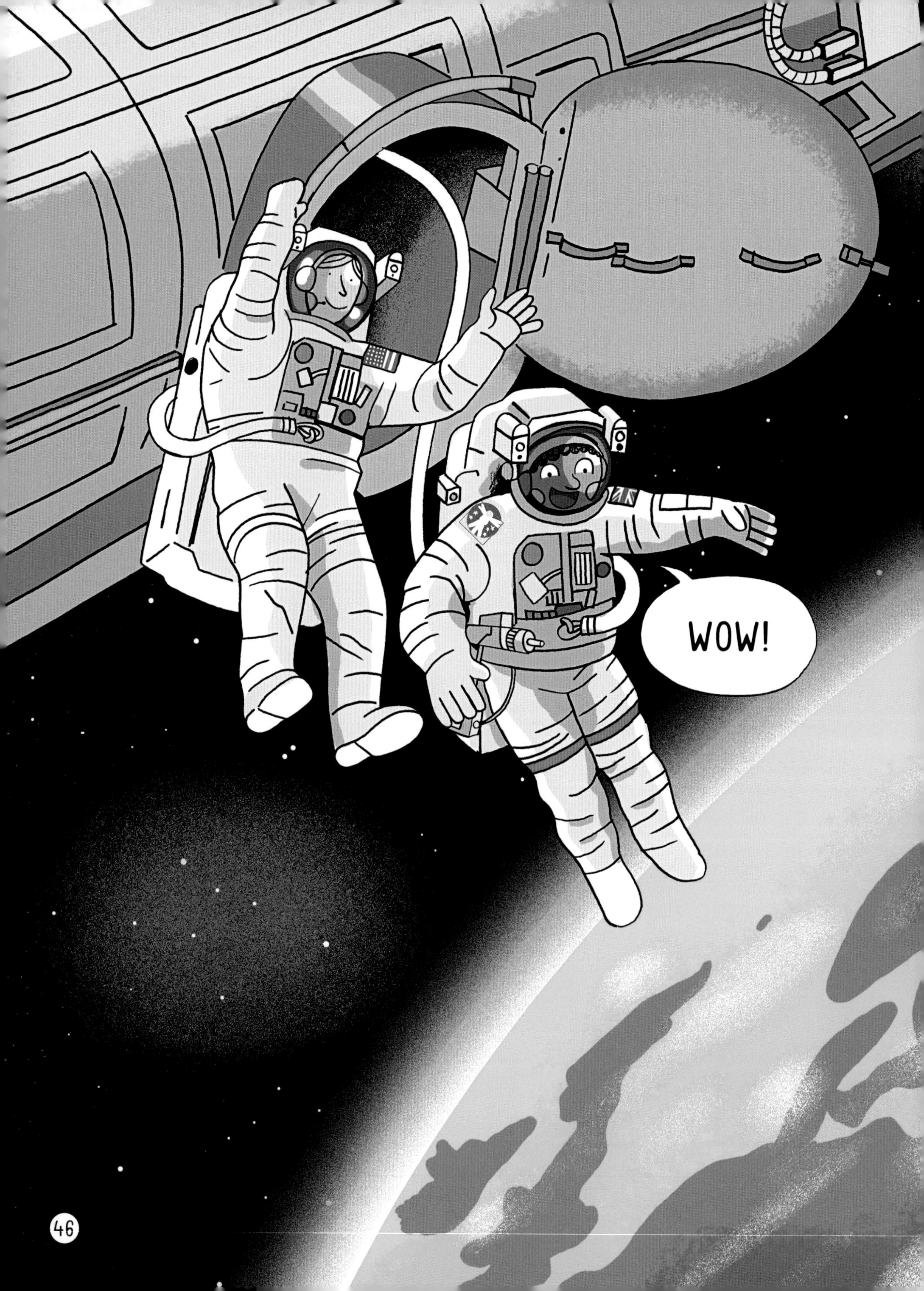
WOW!

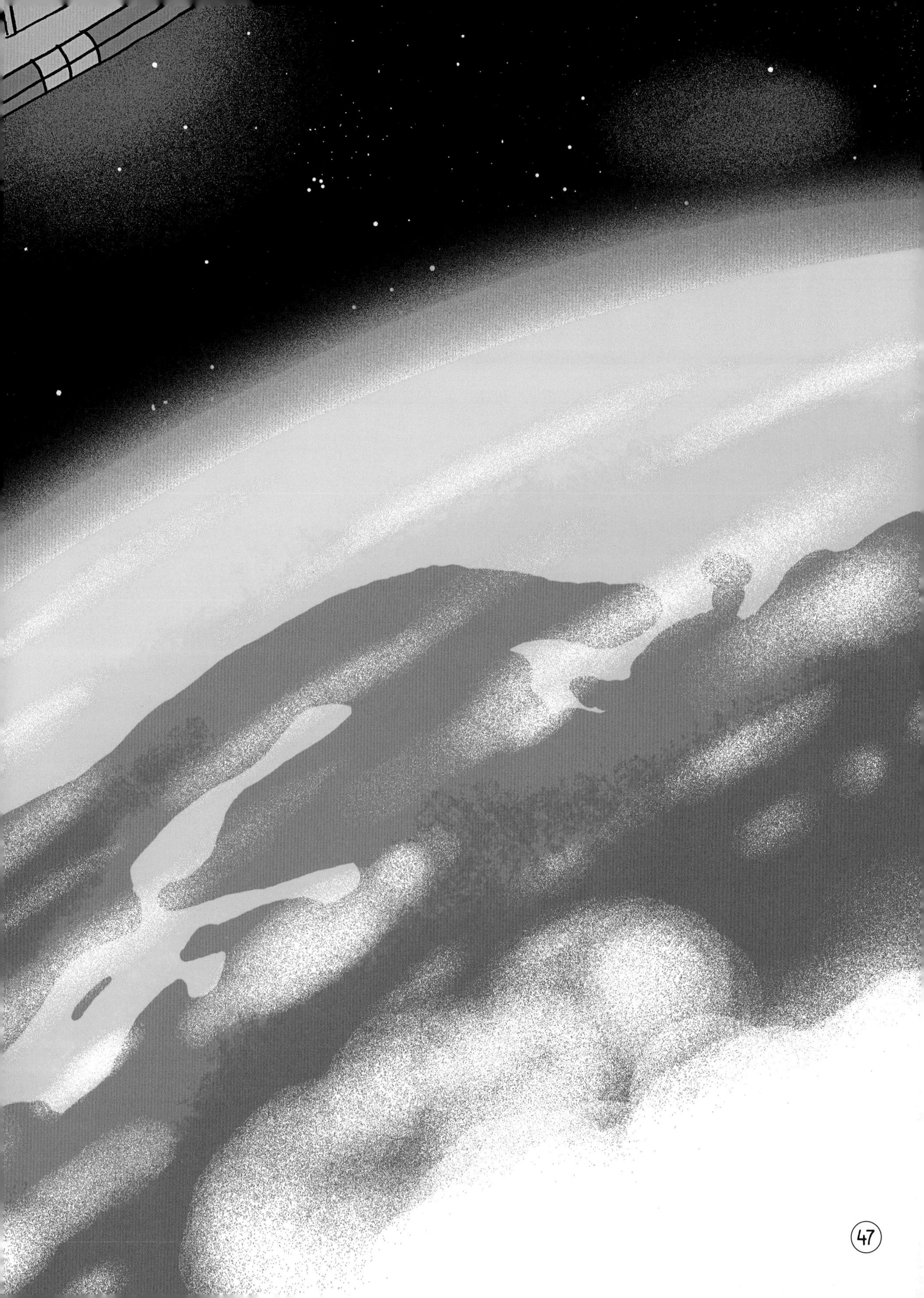

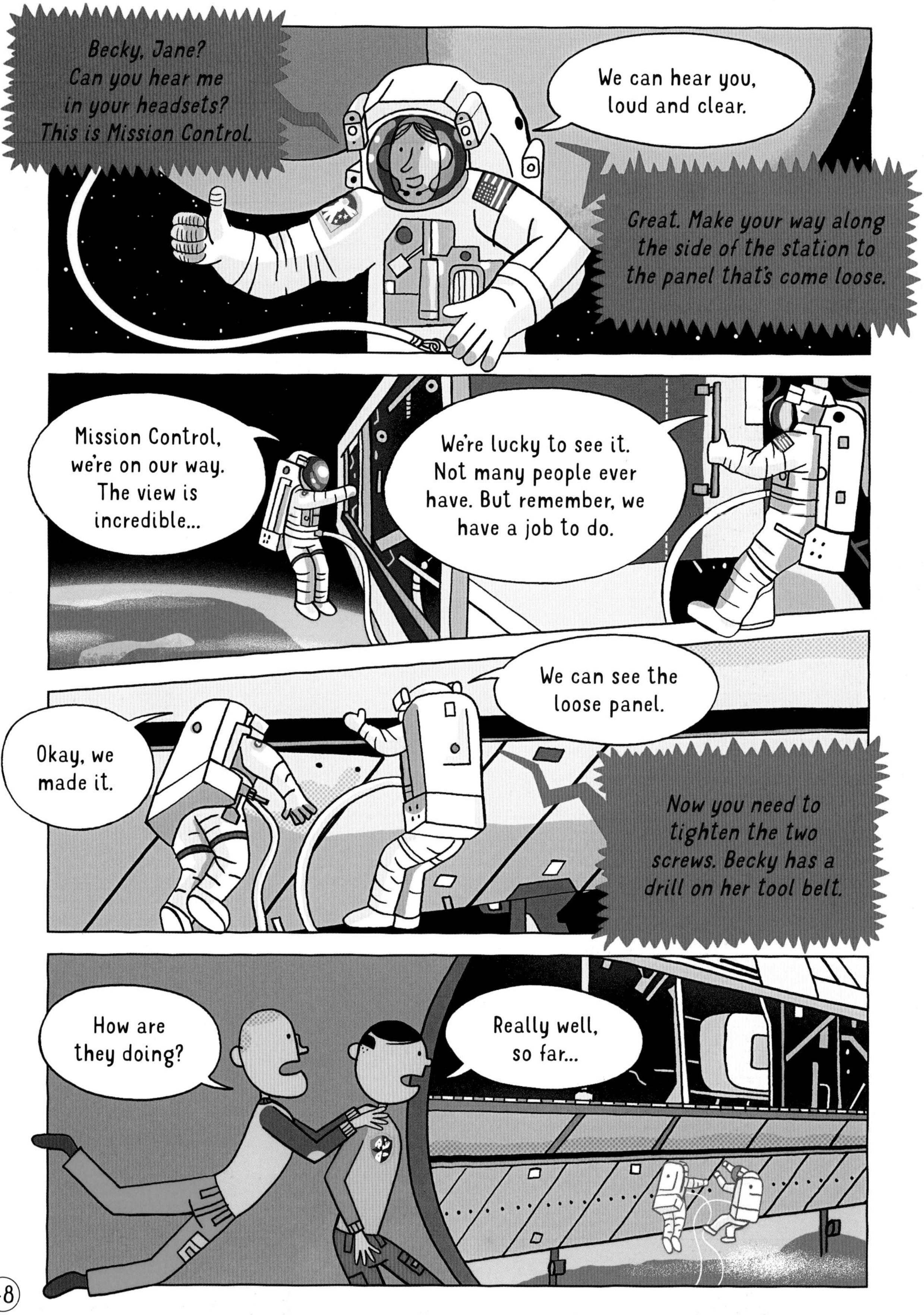
Becky, Jane? Can you hear me in your headsets? This is Mission Control.
We can hear you, loud and clear.
Great. Make your way along the side of the station to the panel that's come loose.
Mission Control, we're on our way. The view is incredible...
We're lucky to see it. Not many people ever have. But remember, we have a job to do.
Okay, we made it.
We can see the loose panel.
Now you need to tighten the two screws. Becky has a drill on her tool belt.
How are they doing?
Really well, so far...

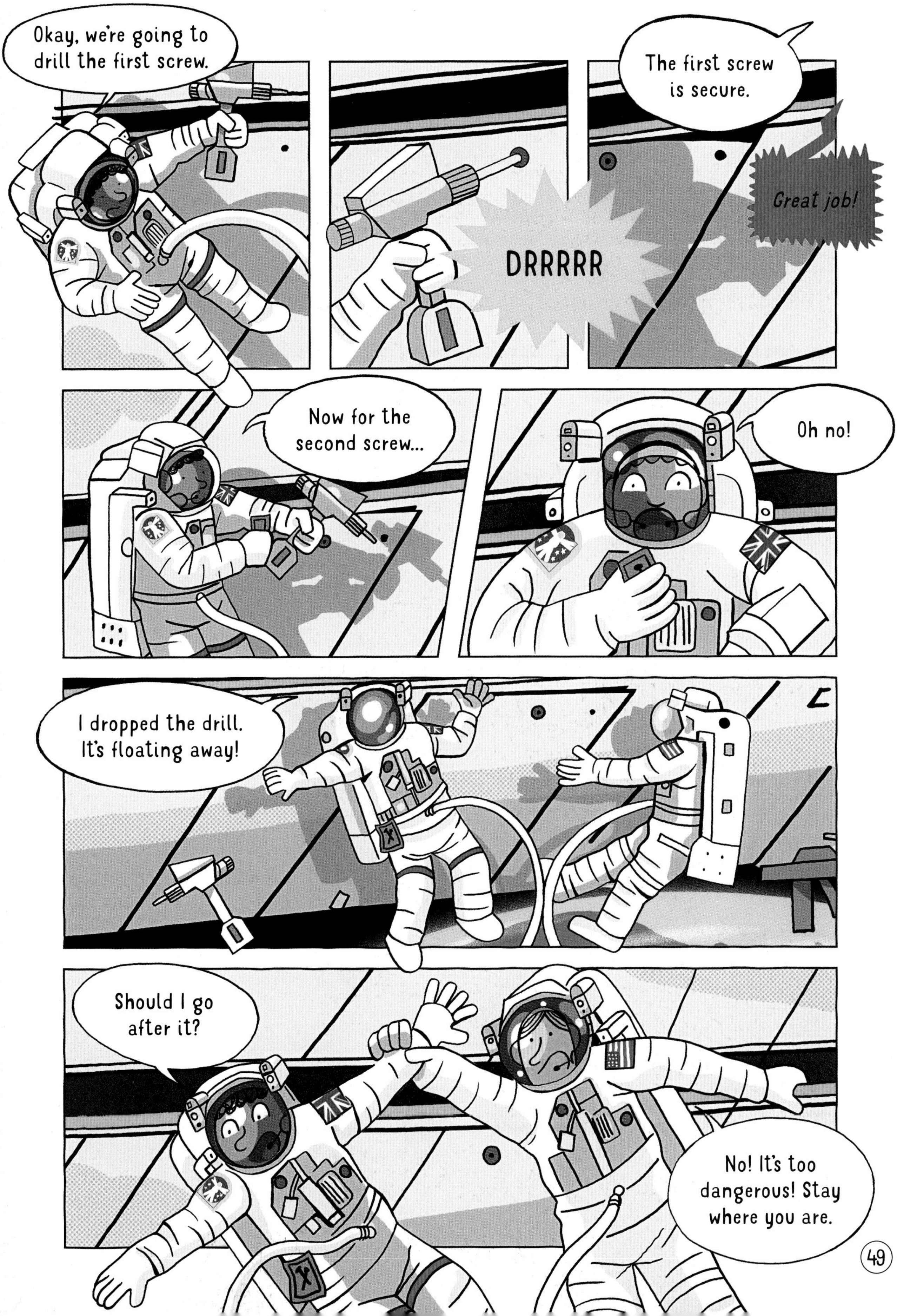
Okay, we're going to drill the first screw.
DRRRRR
The first screw is secure.
Great job!
Now for the second screw...
Oh no!
I dropped the drill. It's floating away!
Should I go after it?
No! It's too dangerous! Stay where you are.

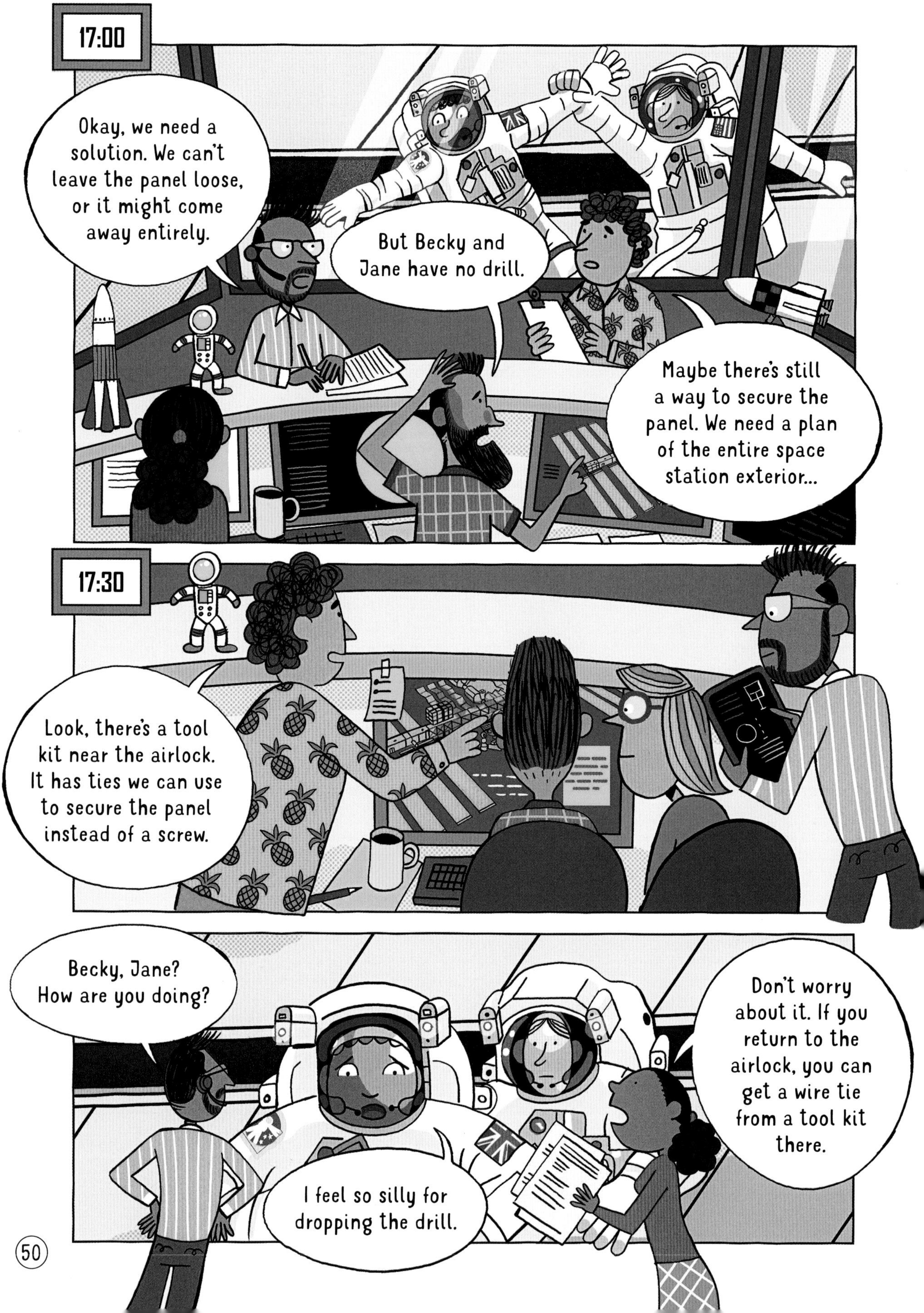
17:00
Okay, we need a solution. We can't leave the panel loose, or it might come away entirely.
But Becky and Jane have no drill.
Maybe there's still a way to secure the panel. We need a plan of the entire space station exterior...
17:30
Look, there's a tool kit near the airlock. It has ties we can use to secure the panel instead of a screw.
Becky, Jane? How are you doing?
I feel so silly for dropping the drill.
Don't worry about it. If you return to the airlock, you can get a wire tie from a tool kit there.

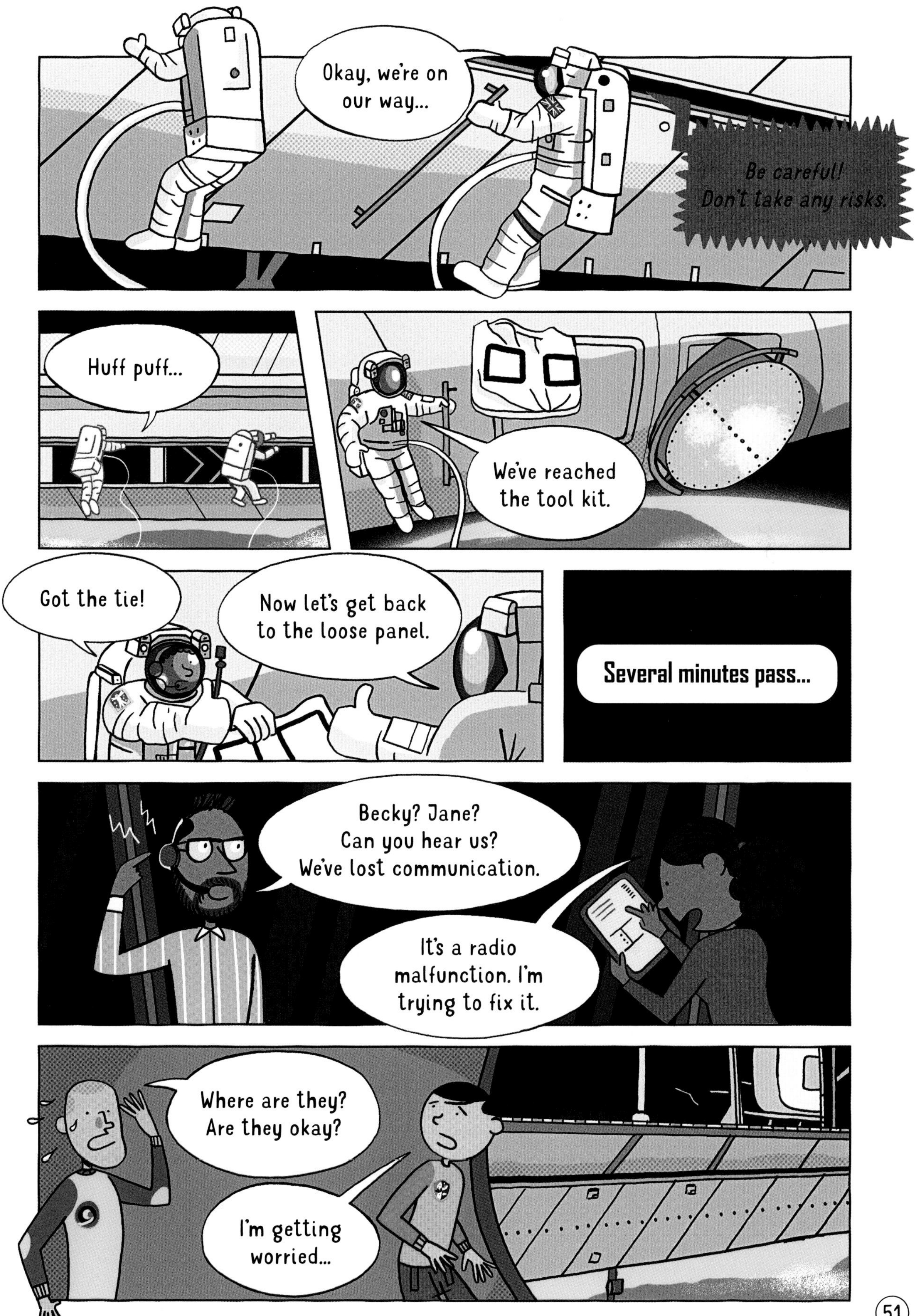
Okay, we're on our way...
Be careful! Don't take any risks.
Huff puff...
We've reached the tool kit.
Got the tie!
Now let's get back to the loose panel.
Several minutes pass...
Becky? Jane? Can you hear us? We've lost communication.
It's a radio malfunction. I'm trying to fix it.
Where are they? Are they okay?
I'm getting worried...

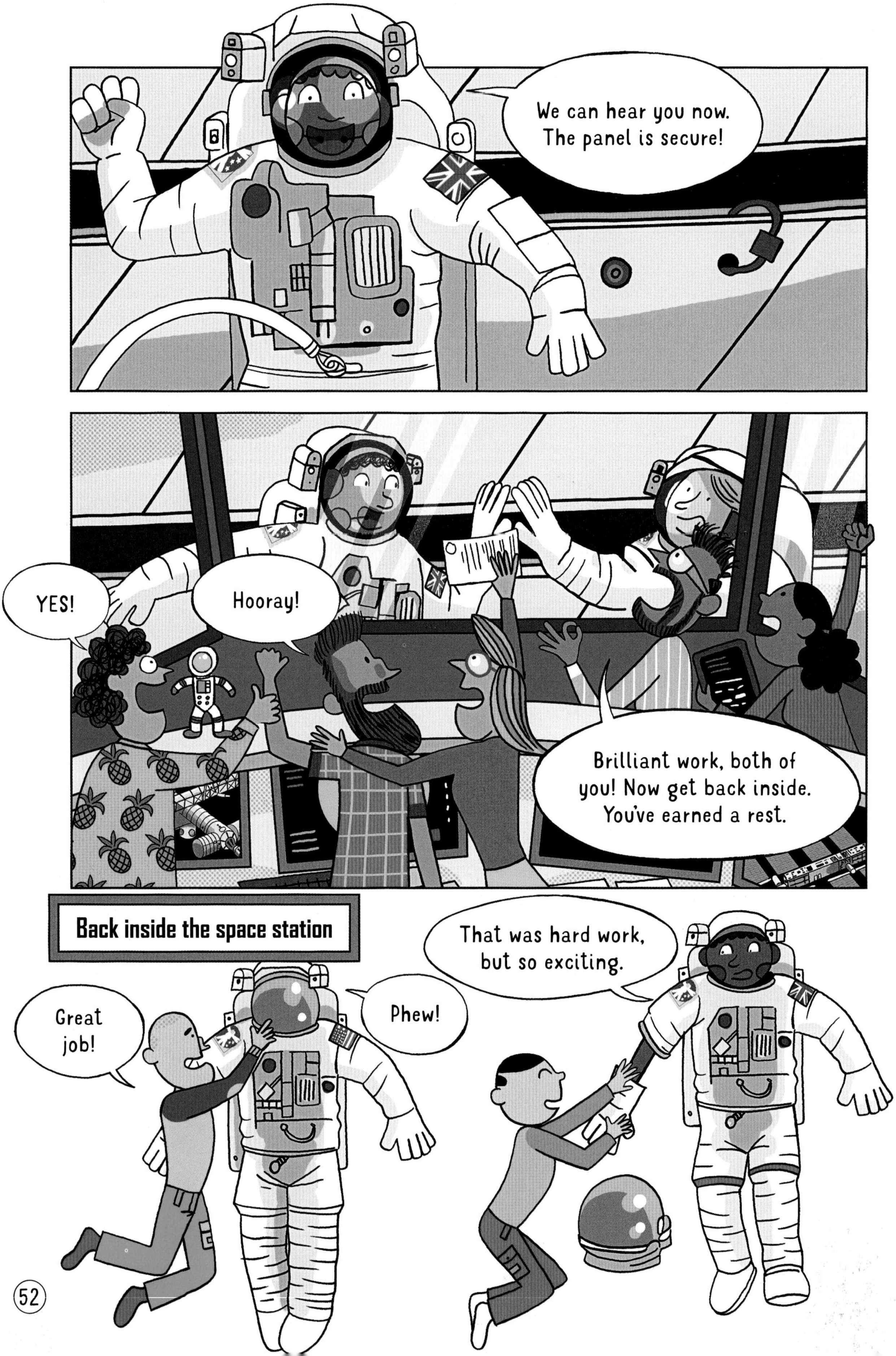

We can hear you now. The panel is secure!
YES!
Hooray!
Brilliant work, both of you! Now get back inside. You've earned a rest.
Back inside the space station
Great job!
Phew!
That was hard work, but so exciting.

20:00 - Relaxing after dinner

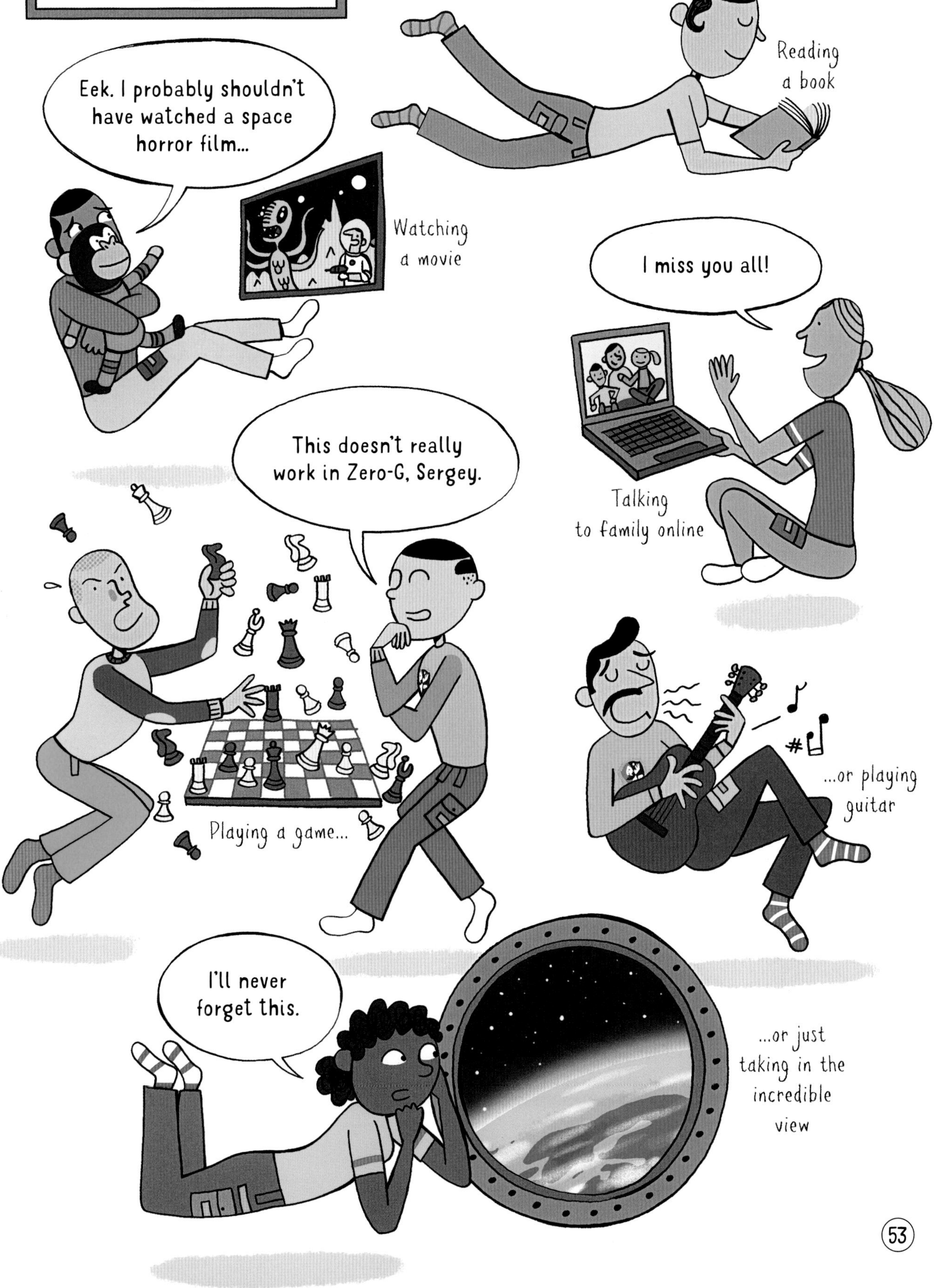
Reading a book
Eek. I probably shouldn't have watched a space horror film...
Watching a movie
I miss you all!
Talking to family online
This doesn't really work in Zero-G, Sergey.
Playing a game...
...or playing guitar
I'll never forget this.
...or just taking in the incredible view

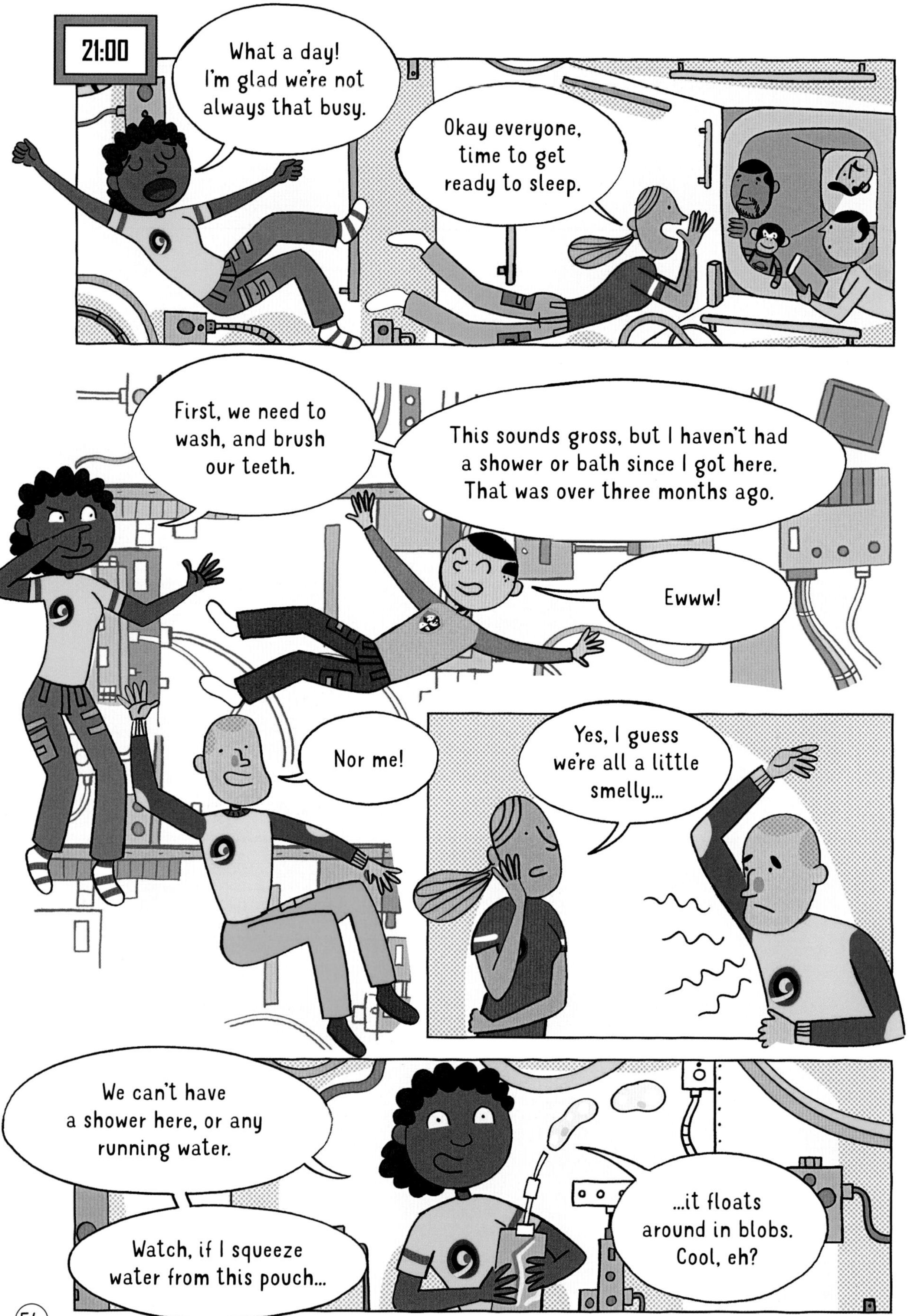
21:00
What a day! I'm glad we're not always that busy.
Okay everyone, time to get ready to sleep.
First, we need to wash, and brush our teeth.
This sounds gross, but I haven't had a shower or bath since I got here. That was over three months ago.
Ewww!
Nor me!
Yes, I guess we're all a little smelly...
We can't have a shower here, or any running water.
Watch, if I squeeze water from this pouch...
...it floats around in blobs. Cool, eh?

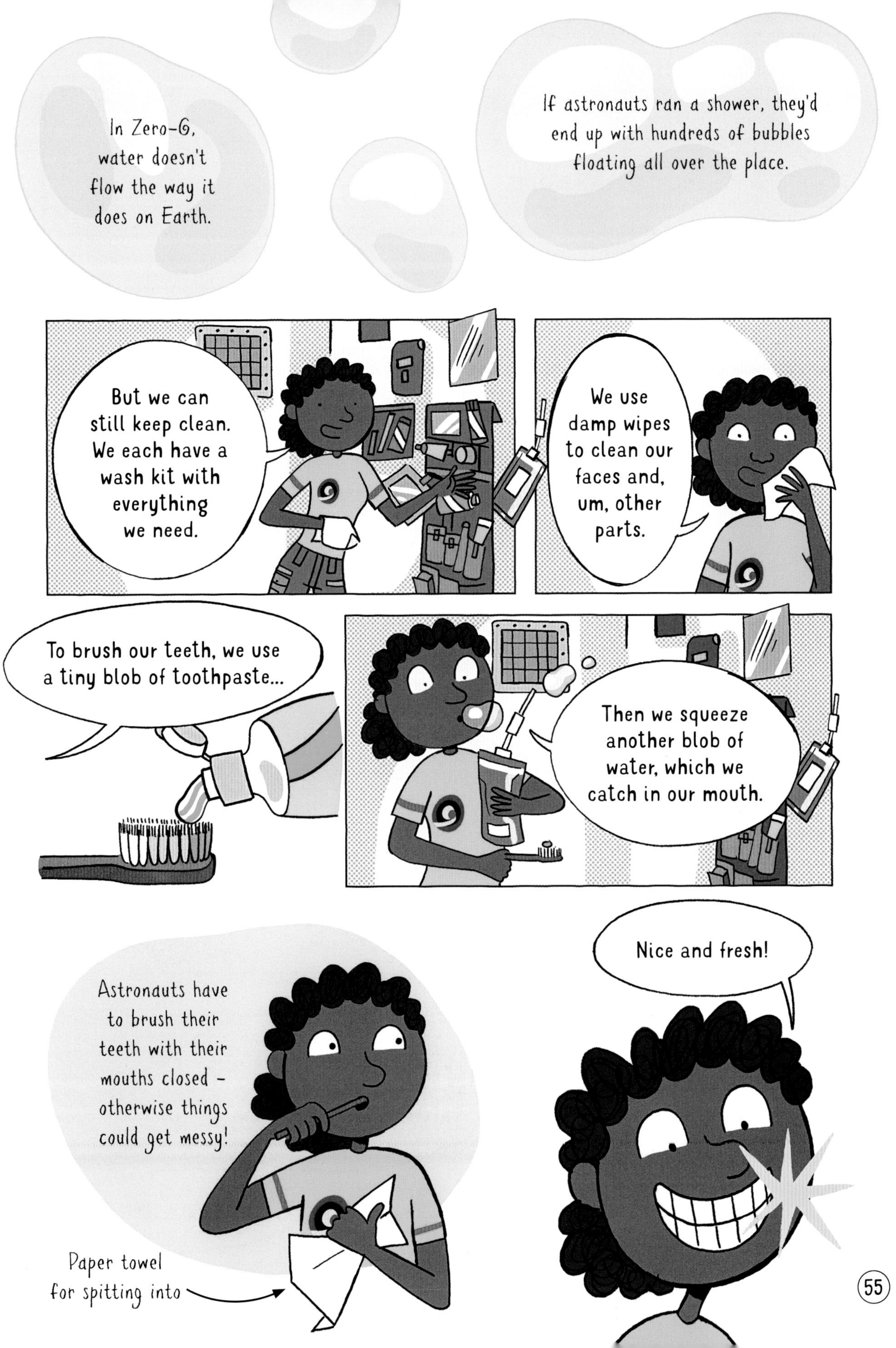
In Zero-G, water doesn't flow the way it does on Earth.
If astronauts ran a shower, they'd end up with hundreds of bubbles floating all over the place.
But we can still keep clean. We each have a wash kit with everything we need.
We use damp wipes to clean our faces and, um, other parts.
To brush our teeth, we use a tiny blob of toothpaste...
Then we squeeze another blob of water, which we catch in our mouth.
Astronauts have to brush their teeth with their mouths closed – otherwise things could get messy!
Paper towel for spitting into
Nice and fresh!

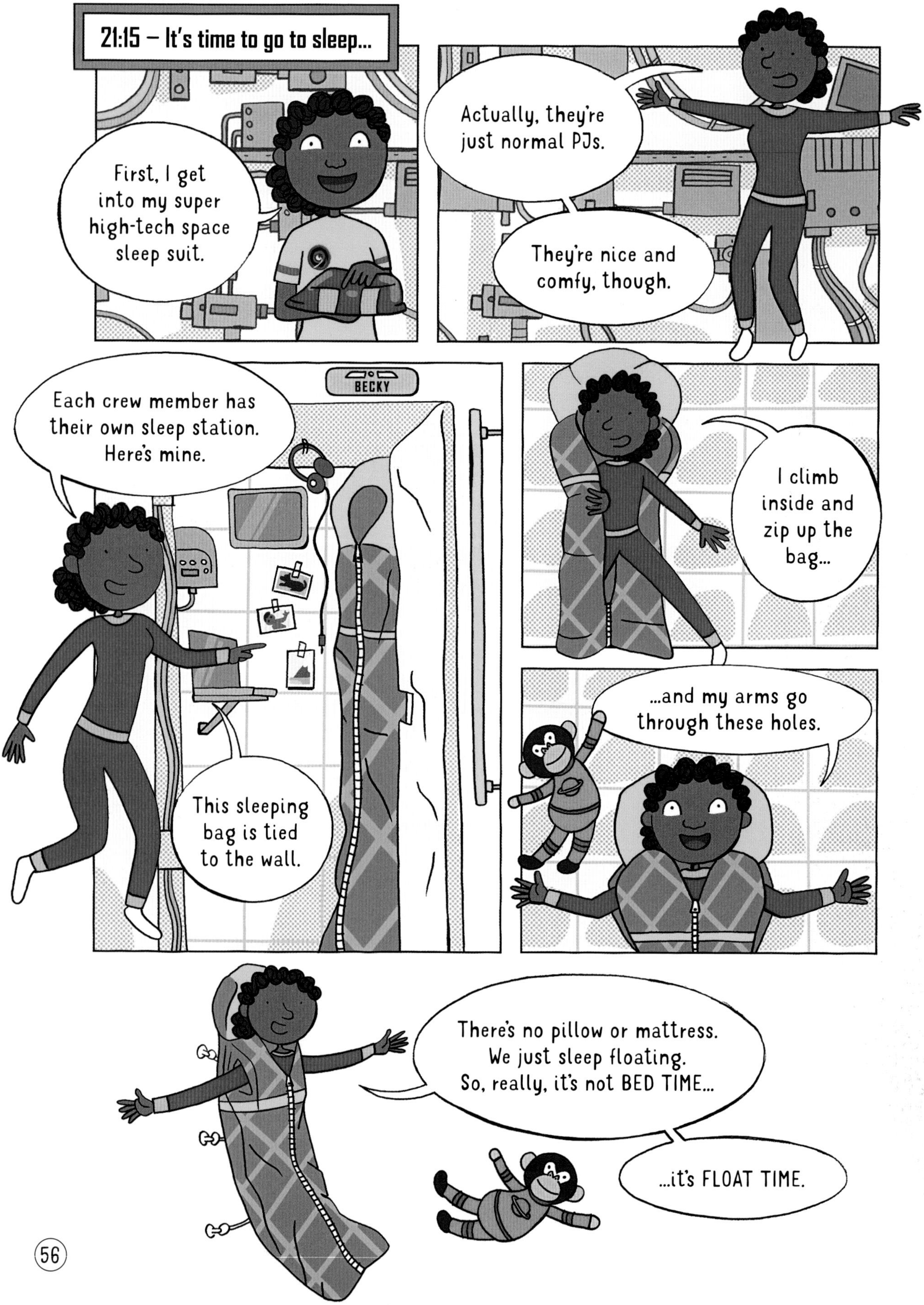
21:15 – It's time to go to sleep...
First, I get into my super high-tech space sleep suit.
Actually, they're just normal PJs.
They're nice and comfy, though.
BECKY
Each crew member has their own sleep station. Here's mine.
This sleeping bag is tied to the wall.
I climb inside and zip up the bag...
...and my arms go through these holes.
There's no pillow or mattress. We just sleep floating. So, really, it's not BED TIME...
...it's FLOAT TIME.

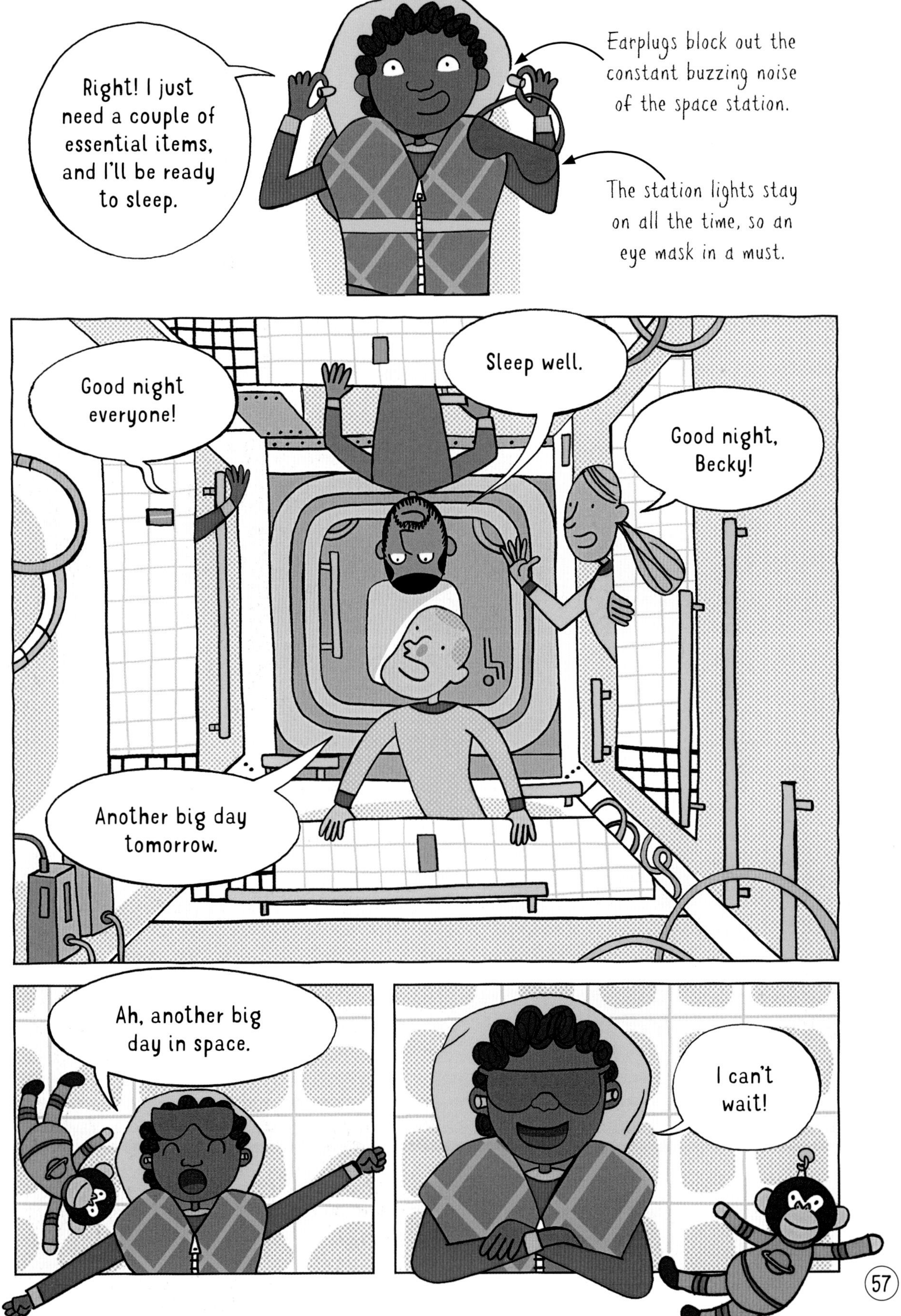
Right! I just need a couple of essential items, and I'll be ready to sleep.
Earplugs block out the constant buzzing noise of the space station.
The station lights stay on all the time, so an eye mask in a must.
Good night everyone!
Sleep well.
Good night, Becky!
Another big day tomorrow.
Ah, another big day in space.
I can't wait!

21:30-06:00

Outer space.
Far above Earth.

The space station drifts.
All is calm. All is quiet...

...until a TERRIBLE snoring noise
echoes across the station.

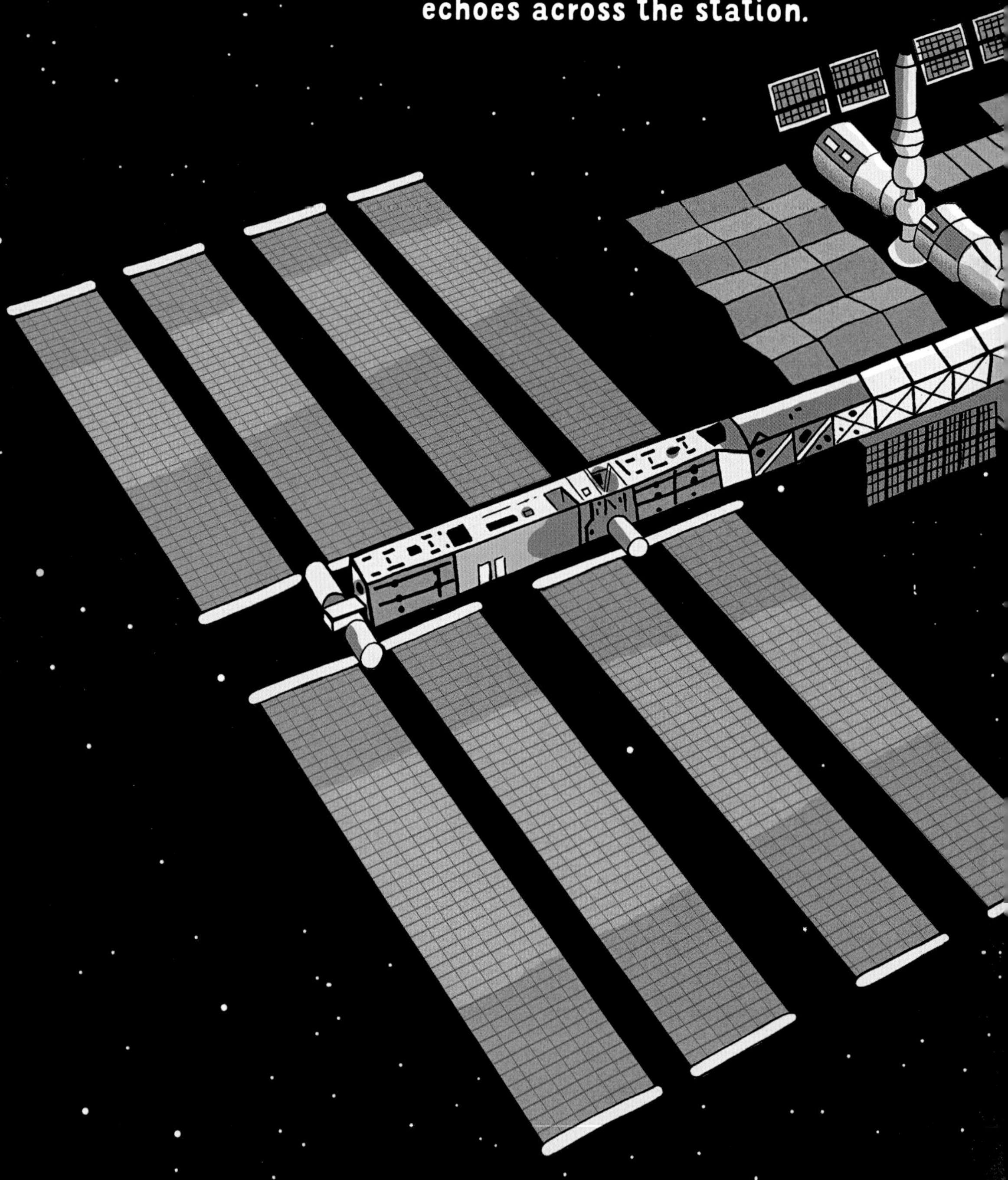

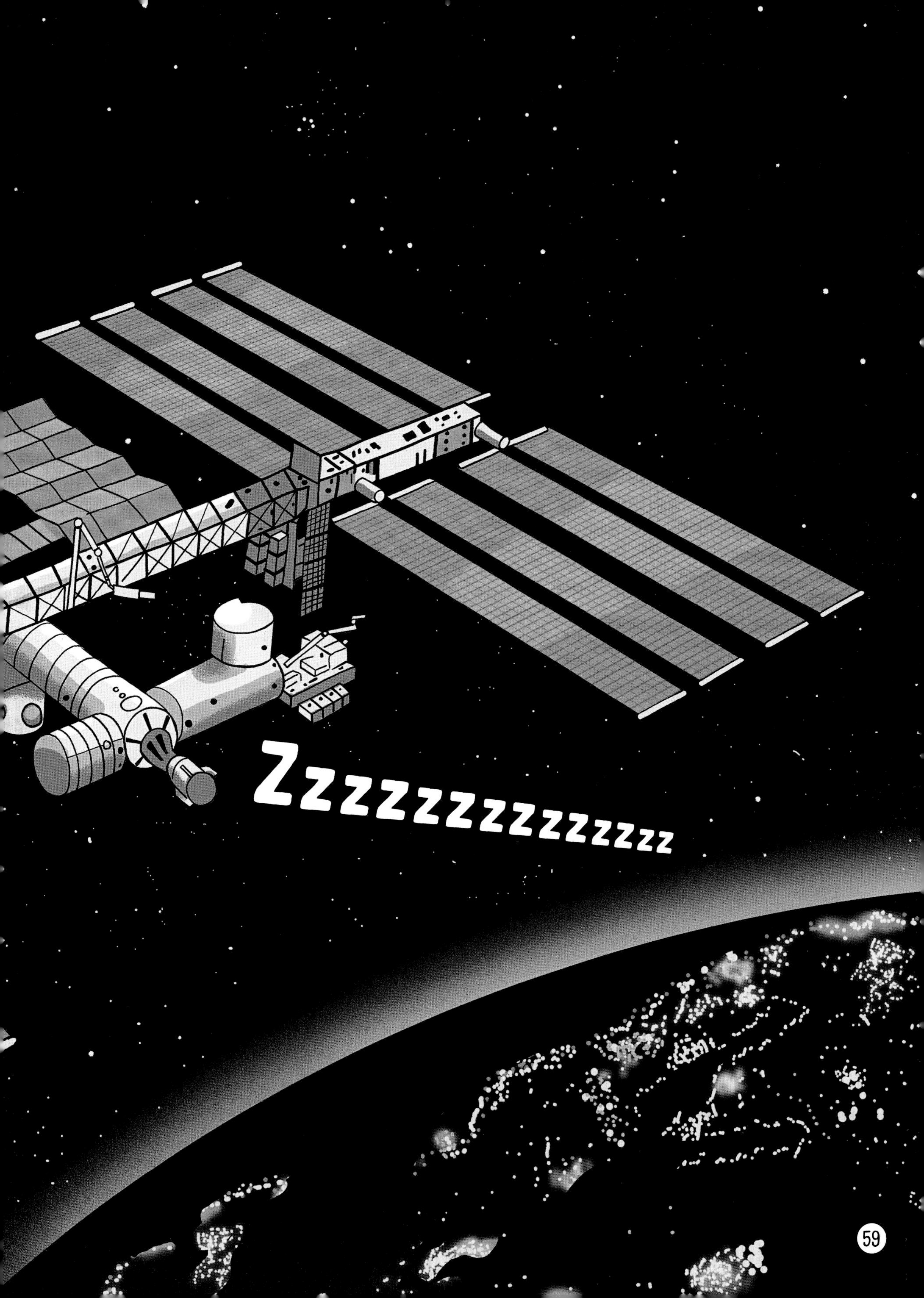
Zzzzzzzzzzzzzz

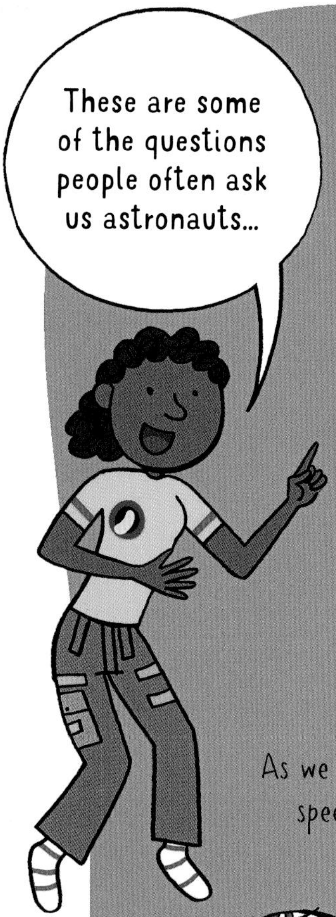
These are some of the questions people often ask us astronauts...

How do you get home from the ISS?

Once my mission is over, after three to six months, it will be time to go home. Usually, we return to Earth with the same astronauts we came to the space station with. For me, that means Jane and Sergey.

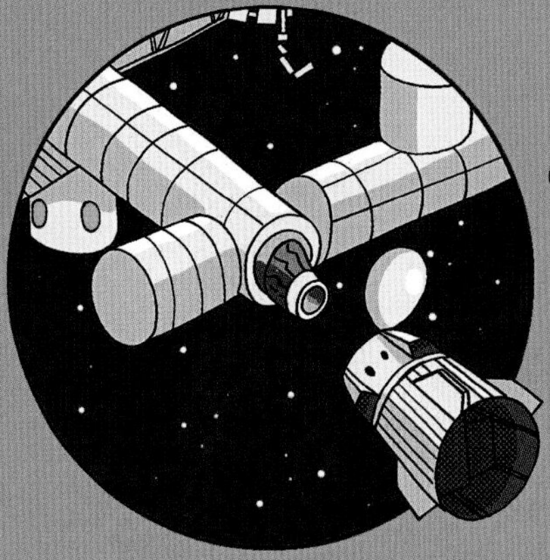

We'll climb into the crew capsule and it will undock from the space station.

Thrusters fire to move us away from the ISS.

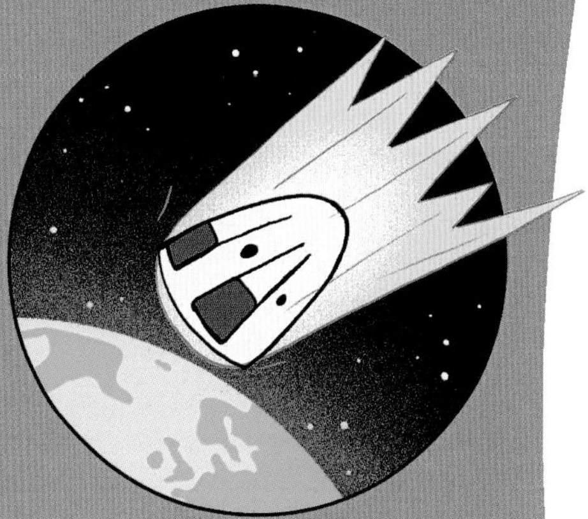

As we re-enter Earth's atmosphere, the capsule's speed creates a lot of heat – even flames.

Don't worry, heat shields on the outside will keep us safe.

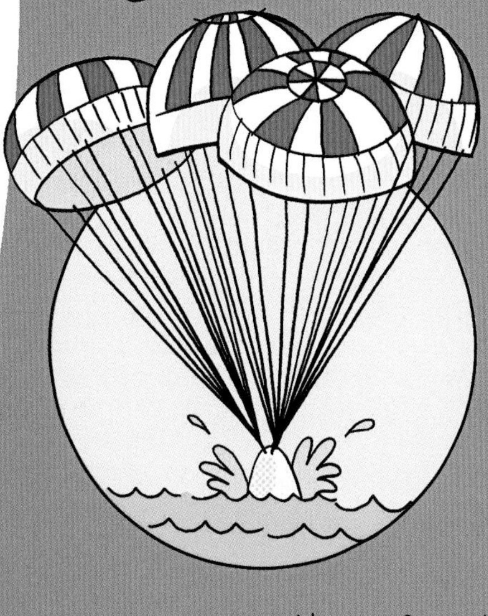

Four huge parachutes slow us down as we descend...

...and splash land in the sea.

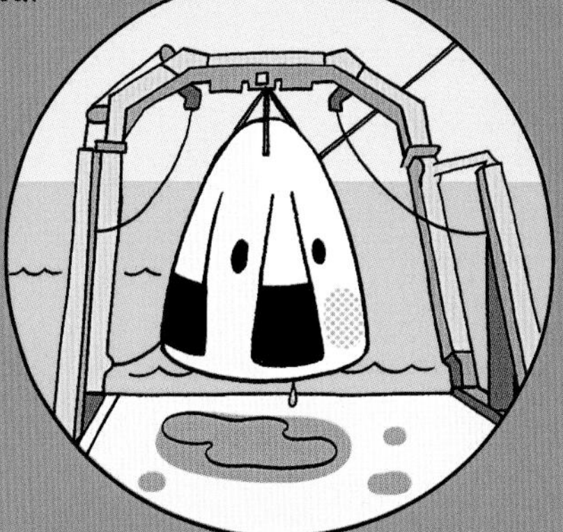

Mission Control will have calculated our path from the space station to Earth. So, boats will be waiting to pick us up.

It will be great to be back on Earth, but also a bit strange. Once you've seen Earth from space, nothing ever feels the same again.

What do you do after you return to Earth?

Some of us return to the ISS on new missions. Others work at a space agency. We use our experience to help other astronauts on their missions, or to train astronauts for future space travel.

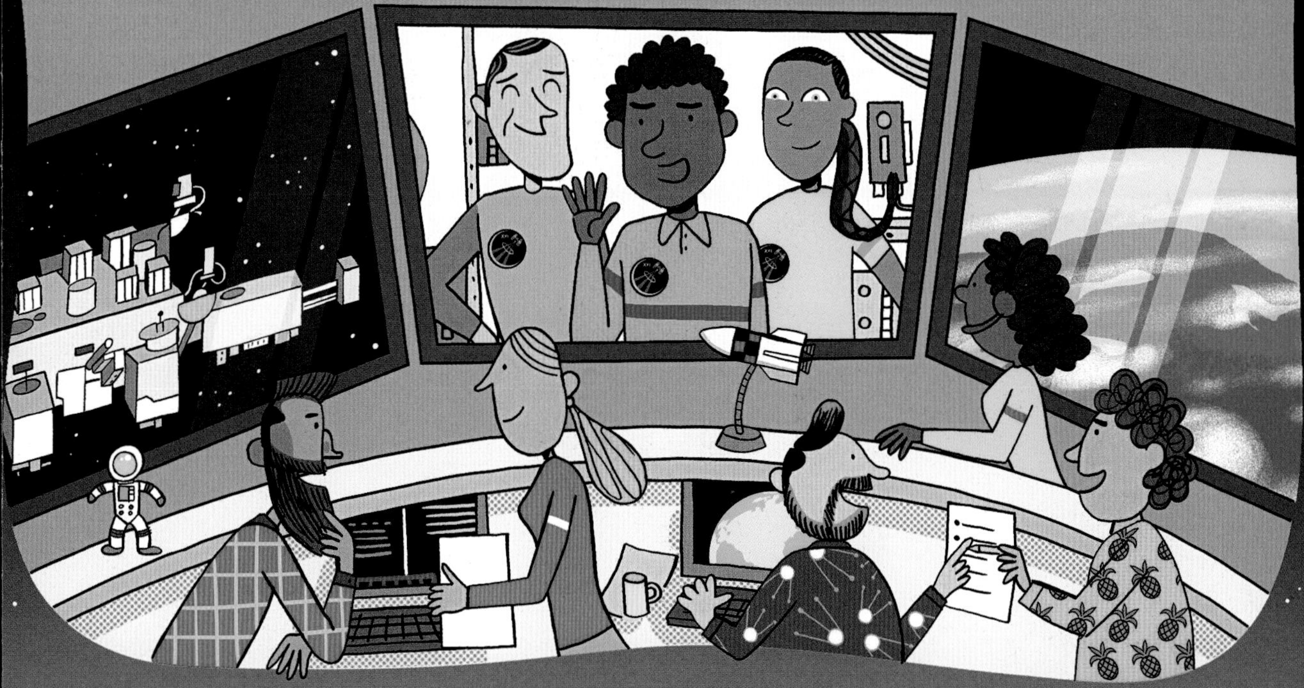

Can I see the ISS from Earth?

You can, but only at certain times and on a clear night. Look for a bright spot of white light passing through the sky. The light will move about as fast as a plane, but it won't flash – if it flashes, it's probably a plane.

The US space agency, NASA, has a website where you can find out exactly when the ISS will pass over where you live.

If you do spot the space station, make sure you wave as we go by!

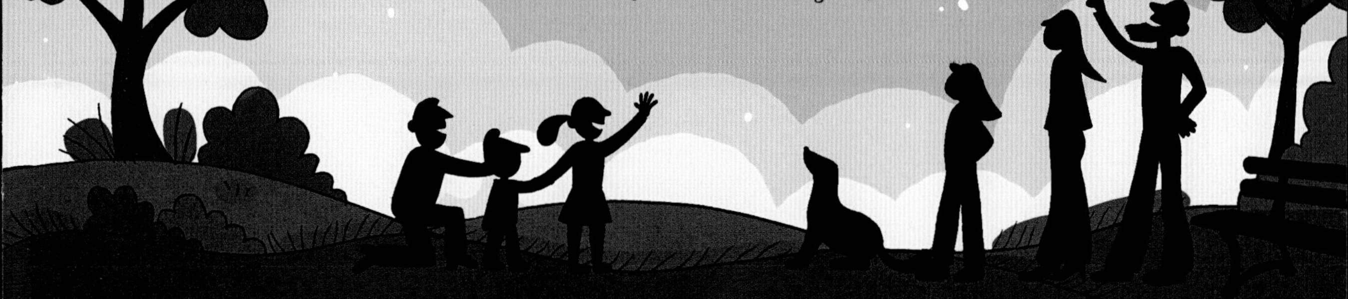

GLOSSARY

This glossary explains some of the words used in this book.

3D PRINTER – A machine that creates physical objects from computer-generated designs.

AIRLOCK – A two-part door that stops air from escaping a spacecraft when an astronaut goes out into space.

ASTEROID – A rock orbiting the Sun.

ASTRONAUT – Someone who goes into space. Known in Russia as a "cosmonaut".

ATMOSPHERE – A layer of gasses held by gravity around a planet.

CARGO VESSEL – A spacecraft used to carry supplies to a space station.

EMU (Extravehicular Mobility Unit) – A type of spacesuit worn by astronauts on spacewalks.

GRAVITY – The force that pulls objects towards each other. The gravity of larger objects is more powerful than smaller ones.

MISSION CONTROL – The group of people on Earth who direct and control missions into space.

MODULE – A large section of a space station.

NODE – A small section of a space station, usually connecting two modules.

NORTHERN LIGHTS – Bright green, red or purple bands of light that appear in the night sky near the North Pole.

ORBIT – The curved path of a smaller object as it moves around a larger object in space, caused by gravity.

PHYSICAL SCIENCE – The science of how materials, fluids and gasses work. Includes physics and chemistry.

SOLAR SYSTEM – A star, such as our Sun, and all the objects that orbit it.

SPACE AGENCY – A government organization in charge of everything to do with space travel.

SPACECRAFT – A vehicle used to travel into and through space.

SPACE STATION – A spacecraft orbiting Earth where astronauts live and work.

SPACEWALK – A mission by an astronaut outside a spacecraft.

UNIVERSE, THE – Everything that exists – all of space and time.

ZERO-G – the "weightless" feeling astronauts experience in space.

INDEX

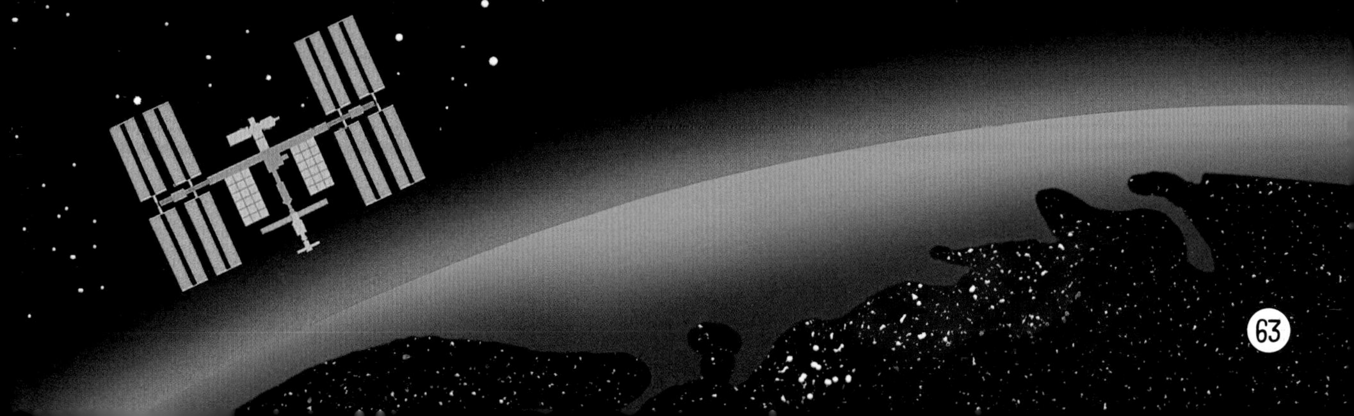

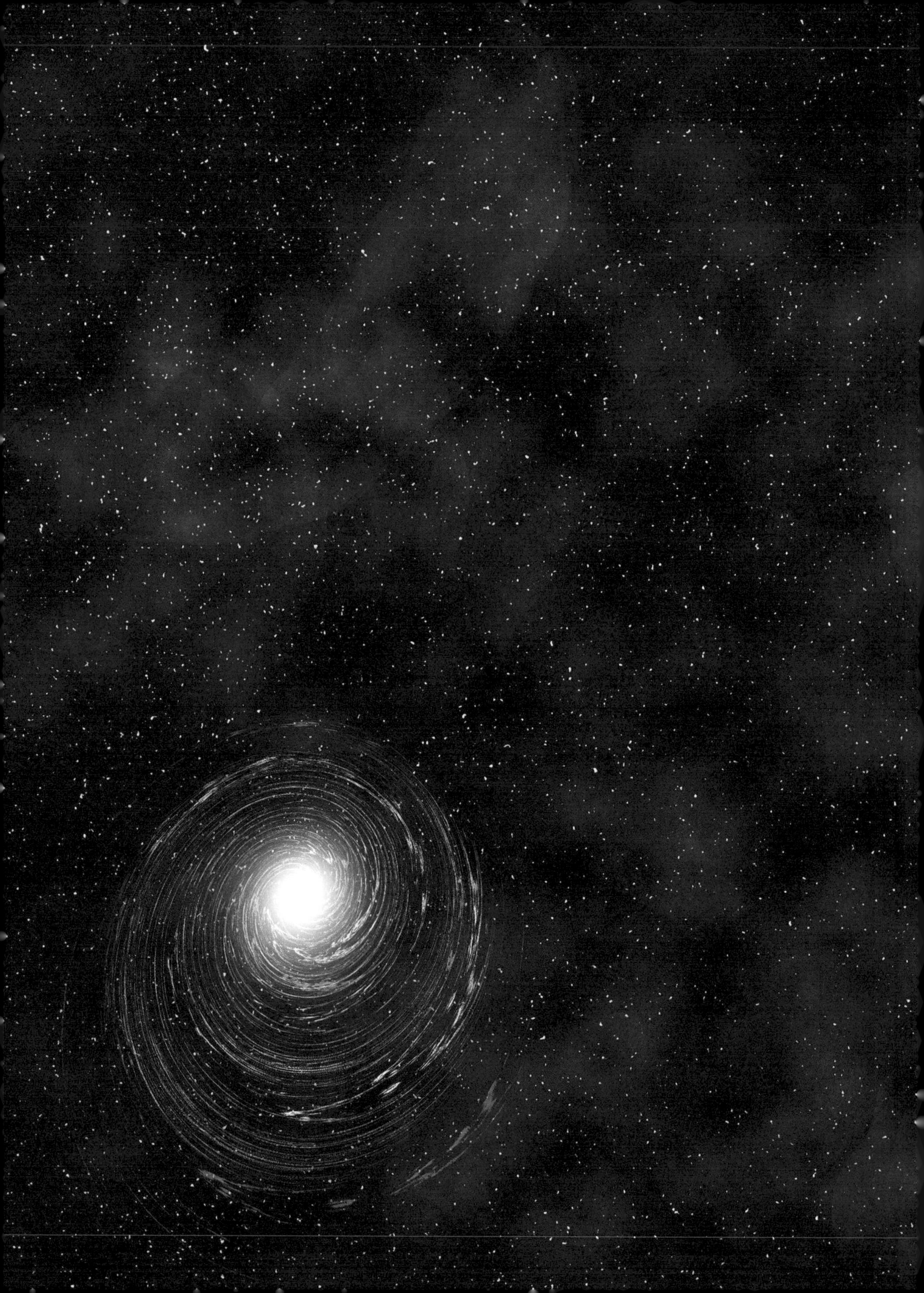